In Rare Form

In Rare Form

A Pictorial History
of Baseball Evangelist
Billy Sunday

W. A. Firstenberger

UNIVERSITY OF IOWA PRESS Iowa City

University of Iowa Press, Iowa City 52242

http://www.uiowa.edu/uiowapress

Copyright © 2005 by the University of Iowa Press

All rights reserved

Printed in the United States of America

Design by Richard Hendel

Cover and title page image: Billy Sunday posing in
his basement at home in Winona Lake, Indiana.
Courtesy Chicago Historical Society, DN-006 9917.

Printed on acid-free paper

Library of Congress
Cataloging-in-Publication Data
Firstenberger, W. A. (William Andrew), 1966–.
In rare form: a pictorial history of baseball evangelist
Billy Sunday / by W. A. Firstenberger.
p.   cm.
Includes bibliographical references and index.
ISBN 0-87745-959-2 (pbk.)
1. Sunday, Billy, 1862–1935.   2. Evangelists—United
States—Biography.   3. Sunday, Billy, 1862–1935—
Homes and haunts.   I. Title.
BV3785.S8F57 2005
269'.2'092—dc22   2005043914
{B}

05 06 07 08 09 P 5 4 3 2 1

Contents

Preface and Acknowledgments vii

Introduction xi

1 Homespun and Cashmere 1

2 Caught on the Fly 11

3 Revival Machine 24

4 For the Love of a Nation 55

5 At Home in Winona Lake 76

Epilogue 104

Appendix A. Revivals and Appearances 111

Appendix B. Conversions 120

Appendix C. Evangelistic Team Members 124

Appendix D. Family Genealogy 127

Notes 139

Bibliography 143

Index 149

Preface and Acknowledgments

The photograph facing this page is an extraordinary image. Billy Sunday is poised to deliver a dramatic blow to the chin of Satan. Sunday used this pose and other active postures regularly in his promotional materials and sermons to illustrate the spiritual combat all individuals fight against sin. Rare among early prints, this photograph is date stamped. Taken as a publicity photograph in March 1918 by the *Chicago Daily News*, this image of Sunday would have been displayed in the newspaper as a cutout figure without any background during his Chicago revival. For our purposes, however, the backdrop remains as salient as his figure, for he is standing in the basement of the family home in Winona Lake, Indiana, in front of a mass of personal possessions. In the foreground we see the public persona of Billy Sunday, but in the background we see his "stuff," the material objects of his past, which, to this date, have still not told their side of the story.

Artifacts and images can only tell a story, however, if they are preserved. For this reason alone, this book is dedicated to the memory of Helen A. Sunday, Billy Sunday's wife, whose singular act in her last will and testament to preserve the Sunday home made possible not only this study but also opened the doors of experiencing the Sunday family story for untold future generations. She made this unselfish gift because thousands of Bible conference attendees enjoyed her personal tour of the family home during the last twenty years of her life; thus she saw the value in keeping the collection intact (fig. 1). She was a woman ahead of her time in numerous ways, and her life and influence upon Sunday are a major focus of this book. To understand the motives of Billy Sunday, one must first comprehend the depth of involvement that Helen Sunday, better known as Nell, brought to the plate. She was his business manager, spiritual counselor, loving mate, and one true friend. Without Nell's abilities or support, it is difficult to imagine Billy Sunday ascending to anything higher than a regionally successful preacher. With Nell

FIGURE I. *Nell "Ma" Sunday, seen here in the Sundays' dining room circa 1945, was the first and best tour guide of the Sunday family home. Image courtesy of the William and Helen Sunday Archives, Grace College, Winona Lake, Indiana.*

at his side, Billy transformed himself into America's great "Baseball Evangelist."

No work such as this occurs without the assistance and guidance from many individuals. The staff at the University of Iowa Press have been of great assistance to me, as a first-time author. Press director Holly Carver took me under her wing and guided me through difficult decisions. Managing Editor Charlotte Wright tended to numerous details, keeping the project on track. Freelance copyeditor Robert Burchfield helped me hone my thoughts into clear statements. During my graduate education at Indiana University, the thesis of which focused on Billy Sunday and served as a germ of an idea for the approach of this book, I was privileged to be under the counsel of Donald B. Marti as my academic adviser, as well as a thesis committee consisting of Daniel V. Olson, Patrick J. Furlong, and Lester C. Lamon. Their guidance and strong encouragement to publish this work greatly bolstered my efforts.

The entire Winona Lake, Indiana, community has likewise been a tremendous source of assistance. I am indebted to Brent Wilcoxson, managing director of the Village at Winona, and Indiana State Museum officials Dale Ogden and Rachel Perry for my appointment as consultant curator to the Billy Sunday Historic Site Museum. These individuals gave me the opportunity to develop this new museum, and without their initial confidence in my ability and continued support over the years, this work would not have been possible. The staff at Morgan Library of Grace College, specifically Director of Library Services William Darr and Associate Director for Public Services Rhoda Palmer, were invaluable to my efforts, as they gave me access to and assistance with the William and Helen Sunday Papers Collection. Steve Grill, director of the Reneker Museum of Winona History, also deserves credit for imparting his unique insights on Billy Sunday's role within the Winona Lake community and opening to me the collections under his care for research. Reneker Museum volunteer Gerald Polman was of particular assistance in helping me document Sunday's appearances and meetings in Winona Lake. Al Disbro kindly volunteered his expertise in photographing the artifacts that illustrate this book. Numerous Winona Lake residents were interviewed, and many of their recollections have found their way into these pages. Perhaps most of all, I wish to thank the more than fifty members of the Billy Sunday Historic Site Museum volunteer corps for their unyielding support in making the Sunday home an invaluable experience for visitors.

I wish to further express my gratitude to the many thousands of visitors who have come to the Billy Sunday Historic Site Museum since it opened full-time to the public in May 2000. Much of the material in the appendixes was included in direct response to visitors' requests for specific statistical information about Billy Sunday's revivals and family. Joseph M. Sanford compiled a wonderful assemblage of postcard images of Billy Sunday and his tabernacles, which he self-published in June 2004. His work led to significant contributions in the appendix addressing Sunday's revivals and appearances. Sunday scholar Jim Lutzweiler has taken on the thankless job of compiling local newspaper accounts of Sunday's revivals, and I discovered many new tidbits of information by using his work as a resource. Longtime Sunday family friend Phyllis P. Leedom of Anderson, Indiana; Billy Sunday Museum volunteer Susan Hight; Rick Sonday of Whitby, Ontario; and Sunday relatives Jim Woods of Huntington, Indiana, and Harry Ashley Sunday of Hood River, Oregon, were of particular assistance in developing the Sunday family genealogy included in the appendixes. Contemporary

Sunday biographers Robert Martin, Wendy Knickerbocker, Lyle Dorsett, Rachel Phillips, and Roger Bruns, along with Craig Bentley of the Columbus Revival Heritage Museum, have all been most encouraging. A very special thanks goes to my friend Brent Grosvenor, who presently travels the country full-time with his wife and two daughters delivering his well-researched, one-man Broadway-style musical *Sunday in Manhattan,* for keeping the Sunday name at the forefront of the American consciousness. My gratitude goes out to Jane Powell Fesler, one of Billy Sunday's last converts in 1935, who granted me more than just an interview but also an opportunity to see at firsthand how this man personally touched the lives of others.

Lastly, I wish to acknowledge the support of my family and friends, who collectively give me purpose and bearings. My Notre Dame brothers, aka the Loons, share greater wisdom than their moniker suggests, and several read drafts of this manuscript and offered indispensable advice. My late father, Bill, started me as a youth down a path in pursuit of truth, a worthy journey that mounts with age. My mother, Fran, has given me more than life; she grounds my perspective in the real world, which is fundamental to the material culture approach. My son, Eric, gave up precious time with Daddy, but not so much time that it revealed I had failed to learn the lessons from Sunday's own family. Finally, this book is for my wife, Lori, whose quiet beauty and grace keep me in a state of eternal wonder and whose love completes the circle of my life.

Introduction

In Rare Form. The phrase seems well suited to Billy Sunday. It was, and still is in certain circles, a colloquial phrase related both to athletes and public speakers being at the top of their game, the peak of their level of performance; therefore it applies directly to Sunday's baseball career and his expressive preaching style. The rarity of the images in this book as well, most of which have never been made public prior to this publication, speaks to the exclusivity of this hidden treasure trove. Finally, and perhaps most significant, this book has been faithfully produced with attention to honoring the decorative details of the Arts and Crafts book-publishing tradition. As such, this book is a revived manifestation of a largely forgotten craft and in its own way is a contemporary artifact "in rare form."

Billy Sunday, America's great "Baseball Evangelist," has been the subject of numerous public reviews through the years in the form of popular magazine articles, editorial cartoons, authorized biographies, and unsolicited scholarly biographies. Perhaps surprisingly, this interest in Sunday has not faded over time, and he remains a popular figure for today's generation. The goal of this work is to provide a new perspective on Billy Sunday by examining the photographic record of his life as well as the landscape, structure, and contents of his home in Winona Lake, Indiana, as if it were a pristine archaeological site. This aim is most unusual for the field of material culture studies for three reasons. First, this book will examine an individual whose thoughts and actions were extensively documented from almost every conceivable angle by the subject himself, his admirers, his critics, contemporary historians, and recent biographers well removed from the emotional halo surrounding Sunday's career. Second, instead of dealing with the tangible issues of a typical archaeological investigation, such as subsistence patterns or technological achievements, Billy Sunday dealt with social issues at the deepest personal levels of human thought, such as the salvation of one's

I contend there should be some visible connection between the thing a man believes in and himself.

—Billy Sunday, in TWENTY YEARS WITH BILLY SUNDAY *by Homer Rodeheaver*

soul. Finally, this book provides a very real departure from most material culture analyses in that it is a biographical account of one individual from the relatively recent past. The interpretations this book offers will therefore be an intimate perspective on one man and one family and the objects and images that reflect their deepest convictions. In many ways, this book provides a litmus test for both the validity and the breadth of material culture studies.

Having artifacts as the primary source of data, one might initially propose an analysis based upon artifact types similar to the manner in which objects are cataloged (that is, furniture, food-processing equipment, household maintenance supplies, and so forth). If the goal was to discuss the organization of museum objects, such a strategy would be entirely appropriate; in this instance, however, artifacts merely serve as the conduit through which the historical figure of Billy Sunday is examined. Therefore, this study is organized according to subjects relevant to Sunday's life: childhood, baseball, evangelism, social issues, lifestyle, and family relations. Each section uses a broad variety of artifacts and images to substantiate interpretations. Also, within each chapter, the consistency between the material evidence and traditional historical interpretations of the same subject is examined.

One other point relates directly to the appropriateness of a material culture analysis of Billy Sunday. Both scholars and the public at large often view the two perspectives of material reality and spiritual reality as incompatible foes. Yet Sunday, in his own words quoted at the beginning of this introduction, admits the verity of an intersection between the material and spiritual worlds. There exists a consensus of written documentation, both in Sunday's own writings and in the first- and second-hand accounts of those who knew and studied him, that he held a very strong antimaterialist view of the world. His unyielding faith in an all-mighty God whose imminent return to this world would result in the final judgment of souls is an interpretation of Sunday's psyche that this study examines in some depth. Taking this spiritual creed as a given at the onset of this examination, one cannot help but presume that Billy Sunday would have had many misgivings about allowing this type of analysis to be applied to his life. For this reason, a Billy Sunday quotation has been inserted at the beginning of each section, providing him a place at the table in this debate. The interpretations realized through this approach gain credibility, however, from the irony that Sunday would have likely dismissed this perspective. If Sunday did indeed devalue the material possessions of life, then this character trait will certainly be reflected in the items he did or did not possess. If his personal actions betray this public conviction, that, too, will be revealed in the material culture. Artifacts do not reveal everything that happened in the past, but they very rarely lie about what they do tell us. Let us now see what they have to say about Billy Sunday.

Chapter 1
Homespun and Cashmere

Few artifacts survive that deal either directly or indirectly with Billy Sunday's childhood. Such a paucity is most certainly predictable considering the impoverished setting in which he was raised. The written facts surrounding his childhood tell of a long chain of broken familial bonds, and the absence of material culture representing this part of his life may be used to reinforce this traditional interpretation. Typically in an archaeological setting, one relies on both the presence of unique artifacts with known dates as well as the absence of commonly found artifacts to assist in interpreting surrounding material that may not carry precise information.[1]

The web of this nation is made from the thread spun in the home. —BILLY SUNDAY SPEAKS!

These techniques may be applied to historic collections, if it is reasonable to assume that the collection, like an archaeological site, has remained largely undisturbed. Indeed, while such an occurrence is very rare, Mount Hood, the Billy and Helen Sunday home in Winona Lake, Indiana, is just such a case. After moving their belongings from Chicago to Winona Lake in 1911, the Sundays added to their possessions, but precious few items were removed. In her last will and testament, Helen Sunday requested that the Mount Hood home remain intact as a shrine to her husband's memory, which perpetuated the integrity of this time capsule. While a few changes in interior room colors or furniture layouts were made over the last ninety years (all of which were easily reversible), the artifact collection has remained intact. Accordingly, with the integrity of this rare collection established, we may proceed with appropriate methods of interpretation.

Farm Boy William Ashley Sunday

When the Devil robs a boy, the last thing he takes from him is what he learned at his mother's knee.—Billy Sunday Speaks!

William Ashley Sunday was born on a farm in Story County, Iowa, November 19, 1862, only thirty-three days before his father died of an undetermined illness while serving in Iowa's Twenty-third Volunteer Infantry Regiment of the Union Army.[2] Billy was sickly and too weak to even sit up or walk on his own for nearly three years, until a traveling doctor gave him a potion made from local roots, leaves, and berries that brought about a complete physical turnaround. Tragedy became a way of life for him during his childhood. In the first ten years of his life, Billy experienced the death of his father, his half-sister's death in a tragic bonfire accident, and the deaths of four aunts, an uncle, and his beloved grandmother, all from tuberculosis. His oldest brother, Albert, was kicked in the head by a mule and eventually had to be institutionalized.[3] This wave of hardship and death would leave a lasting mark on Billy that helped to shape his later views on salvation and heaven.

Billy's sorrows continued in 1874 at the age of twelve, when he and his older brother Ed were sent to the Iowa Soldier's Orphan Home.[4] Some mystery surrounds the sending of these two boys to the orphanage since Billy's grandfather, Squire Martin Cory, lived near the family and was financially able to support the small family. Yet he stood by and allowed the two boys to be sent 130 miles away to the Glenwood orphanage. Recent scholarship has pieced together the most likely scenario that led to this family hostility. A good deal of conflict apparently existed between Martin Cory and his daughter, Mary Jane (Jennie), Billy's mother (fig. 2). Jennie's second husband, James M. Heizer, had financially abused his position as guardian of the Sunday boys. He not only confiscated their Civil War pension appropriations but also placed Cory liable for the debt since Cory had agreed to serve as Heizer's bondsman when Heizer had become the children's guardian. When Heizer abandoned the family in 1871, Cory was left holding the bag for the misappropriated pensions and other debts. The combination of monetary strife and his frustration with his daughter's choices in men probably led to the unfortunate situation of the Sunday children being caught in the middle.[5]

The result of this family tension, coupled with Jennie Cory's inability to support her children, was the sending of her two youngest sons to an orphanage for the offspring of fallen Union soldiers. While the separation from his mother was traumatic, it was probably the single biggest turning point in young Billy's life. Besides receiving superior schooling in the basic skills of reading, writing, and arithmetic, he learned valuable social skills from living with countless other children. During those long years away from home, he learned to defend himself, take pride in

FIGURE 2. *Mary Jane (Jennie) Cory Sunday Heizer Stowell, Billy's mother, standing in front of the log cabin in Story County, Iowa, where Billy Sunday was born. This circa 1885 photograph is the only known image of Billy's half brother, who Jennie had with her last husband, George Stowell. Image courtesy of the William and Helen Sunday Archives, Grace College, Winona Lake, Indiana.*

FIGURE 3.
*Billy Sunday just as he
was beginning his baseball
career in 1884 at the age of
twenty-two. This is the
earliest known photograph
of Sunday. Image courtesy
of the William and Helen
Sunday Archives, Grace
College, Winona Lake,
Indiana.*

his work, and discipline his behavior. While as a youth he did not completely internalize the message of the sermons he heard, the orphanage regularly exposed the children to Bible lessons. Lastly, he developed his physical prowess for speed. In particular, he learned the basics of the game of baseball (spoken as two words: "base ball," in his youth) and how his sprinter's quickness could make him a valued asset on almost any team. These learned and developed skills served him immediately when he returned to live on the farm in 1876 (fig. 3).

While the scarcity of childhood artifacts in Sunday's possession remains consistent with the written tradition that he was brought up in an economically depressed household, the handful of surviving childhood-era artifacts do yield a few insights. Two medals and four badges from the Civil War Survivors Association were found in the master bedroom dresser (fig. 4). These items were given only to the widows and children of fallen soldiers at Grand Army of the Republic encampments and other similar veterans' meetings. These six objects most certainly

FIGURE 4. *Clockwise from upper left: framed sampler of Cory family,* Roster and Record of Iowa Soldiers in the War of the Rebellion, *salt print of Squire Martin Cory, two Grand Army of the Republic survivor badges, nineteenth-century bugle horn. Items courtesy of the Billy Sunday Historic Site Museum, Winona Lake, Indiana.*

belonged to Billy's side of the family, since no one in Nell's immediate family is known to have perished in the war, although her father, William Thompson, did serve in the Fifty-first Infantry Regiment of Illinois. A child's bugle-type horn from the time period of Billy's youth could well have been his and may also have been a reminder of his father who died for the Union cause. These artifacts, which point toward a period of sorrow and want in young Billy's life, of course also reflect national pride, the fight for moral values, and America's claim to the title of "God's chosen country," themes that would be carried through to his evangelical career. These values are verified by his ownership of a bound volume of the *Roster and Record of Iowa Soldiers in the War of the Rebellion.* Billy did not own the entire set, only volume 3, which contained his father's listing, suggesting that this book was an object that he actively sought to possess.

A cross-stitch sampler (fig. 4) with the names of his grandparents on his mother's side (Martin and Mary Cory), his grandfather's second wife (Charlotte Cory), his father and mother (William and Jennie "Sundy" — the "a" left out due to lack of space), and his mother and her second husband (Matt and Jennie Heizer) suggest that this item is from the brief period of time in Billy's life after his mother remarried but before 1874 when she was forced to send Billy and his brother to the orphanage. This memento, probably created by his mother, atypically chronicles a succession of wives.

A salt-print photograph of Billy's grandfather Squire Martin Cory was also likely passed down to Billy from his mother. While Billy always professed to hold his family in the highest regard, and indeed his mother did live with Billy and Nell seasonally at Mount Hood before her death in 1916, little material culture exists to reflect strong familial bonds. Neither handmade crafts from mother to son nor evidence of lavish gifts of a successful preacher to his elderly mother are to be found in the collection. The scarcity of photos of his mother or his brothers reaffirms the paucity of early family artifacts, suggesting erratic, fragmented relationships with kin. This interpretation is entirely consistent with documented accounts of Billy's ongoing frustrations in relationships with his grandparents, stepfathers, and siblings.

For all the emphasis made in biographical accounts of Billy's experiences at the Iowa Soldier's Orphanage, not a single artifact has been uncovered in the Sunday home representing this time in his life. Written accounts document that Billy's brother Ed, as an adult, returned to the orphanage to work there as a carpenter and watchman for many years, further suggesting a continuation of the link between this institution and the Sundays.[6] During Sunday's campaigns, much was made in the newspaper coverage of this difficult hurdle in his life, and while he apparently visited the Reynolds Presbyterian Orphanage in Albany, Texas, in 1918, where the children gave him a bull's horn presentation trophy, the lack of any items representing the Iowa orphanage remains a mystery. This absence of material remains does not necessarily suggest that the written accounts are inaccurate. However, it is curious that physical evidence of the Iowa Soldier's Orphanage connection is so weak, considering how much material culture in the home reflects other institutions that reputedly had positive impacts on Billy's life, such as the Pacific Garden Mission, the Young Men's Christian Association (YMCA), or major league baseball.

City Girl Helen Amelia Thompson

Better die an old maid, sister, than marry the wrong man.
—The Real Billy Sunday (*Brown*)

Helen Amelia Thompson was born in Dundee, Illinois, on June 25, 1868, but the family soon moved to Chicago after her birth. Nell's parents, William and Ellen Thompson, were immigrants from the Scottish highlands. A successful dairy businessman and staunch Presbyterian, William Thompson was able to provide well for his family, giving Nell many luxuries in her youth that would have been inconceivable to Billy Sunday. She attended private schools and received lessons in music and the arts. At the time she met Billy, both were involved in serious relationships bordering on official engagements of marriage: Billy with a woman named Clara, whom he had been seeing for three years in Iowa before beginning professional baseball, and Helen with a churchmate, Archie Campbell.[7] Not at all impressed with the country bumpkin baseball player Billy Sunday, William Thompson strongly discouraged their courtship, but to no avail. Billy eventually won over William Thompson due in no small part to considerable backing from Nell's mother. After their marriage, which took place in the Thompson home, Billy and Nell lived for twenty-two years in the brownstone at 64 Throop Street directly adjacent to the site of their wedding (fig. 5).

Several of Nell Thompson's artifacts support the interpretation that this couple came from decidedly different backgrounds. A tintype of herself with two teenage friends, a fancy velvet-covered autograph album filled with good wishes from high school classmates, and several early cabinet photos of herself and family members indicate that Nell had a stable home life and a set of parents who could provide well for their children (fig. 6). Included in the Sunday home's collection are several fine examples of Victorian-period Eastlake-style furniture that originally belonged to the Thompson family. Two three-piece sets of Victorian furniture, both of which consist of two side chairs and a platform rocker, all came from the Thompson household. The most elaborate of these hand-me-downs is an Eastlake settee with decorative birds of inlaid wood. Nell recalled in her memoirs how she and Billy did their courting on this settee in her mother's parlor in the 1880s.[8] Her schoolbooks, such as *Gray's School and Field Book of Botany* and *The Packard Commercial Arithmetic*, reveal that Nell received much more advanced schooling than Billy. The latter text also foretold her invaluable role as

FIGURE 5. *The Thompson family in front of their brownstone home at 62 Throop Street, Chicago, circa 1885. Nell Thompson (Sunday) is shown sitting on the railing in the center. Image courtesy of the William and Helen Sunday Archives, Grace College, Winona Lake, Indiana.*

future business manager of the grand revival campaigns. Also from this period are Nell's oil paintings, a collection of a dozen paintings of various subjects. The original box of tube paints from this early time in her life still survives in the family collection. Nell's mother hired an itinerant French artist to give her daughter lessons, and Nell painted a wide variety of subjects as exercises, including still lifes of fruit and floral arrangements, a seascape, several rural landscapes, a western mountain landscape, and her own interpretation of the well-known painting *Pharaoh's Horses*.[9] The rural landscapes are particularly revealing in that they represent Nell's vision of a lifestyle so different from her own yet strikingly similar to Billy's childhood experiences (fig. 6). One wonders if Billy chuckled under his breath when he observed in Nell's rural landscapes fat chickens, full bowls of ripe fruit, and well-tailored clothes, when he often recalled that life on the hardscrabble farm included hunger and homespun pants that "couldn't tell whether I was coming or going."[10] Unlike Billy, Nell Thompson was a child born with a silver

FIGURE 6. *Clockwise from the top: rural landscape oil painting by Nell Thompson (Sunday), tintype of Nell with friends, box of tube paints, two H.A.T. monogrammed silver spoons,* The Packard Commercial Arithmetic. *Items courtesy of the Billy Sunday Historic Site Museum, Winona Lake, Indiana.*

spoon in her mouth. She even had two spoons from which to choose, a set of two Towle Company silver-plated spoons bearing her monogram, "H.A.T."

The Sunday home yields an interesting assemblage of artifacts from 1886 to 1890, a period that includes Billy's conversion to Christianity, his courtship of Nell, and the first years of their marriage before he left baseball. Nell's copy of the *Hymnal of the Presbyterian Church in Canada* provides an important link between this future husband and wife and the Presbyterian denomination. She was very active in Chicago's Jefferson Park Presbyterian Church, where her parents were members. She sang in the choir, vigorously participated in the Christian Endeavor Society, and held the position of superintendent of the Intermediate Department of Sunday Schools for the church.[11] *Index to the Bible*, given to Nell by her aunt Sue in 1887, further suggests that she took a very serious, scholarly approach to her faith. By contrast, Billy was a newly formed Christian, and although his mother was a staunch Methodist, Billy openly admitted that his foundation in the Presbyterian denomination was due to Nell. He stated on several occasions, "She was a Presbyterian, so I am a Presbyterian. Had she been a Catholic, I would have been a Catholic — because I was hot on the trail of Nell."[12] But Billy did have competition. Three books by Oliver Wendell Holmes, *The Poet at the Breakfast-Table*, *The Professor at the Breakfast-Table*, and *The Autocrat of the Breakfast-Table*, were Christmas gifts in 1886 from Nell's longtime steady boyfriend, Archie Campbell. Billy Sunday was nothing if not persistent. He recalled in an autobiographical account that Nell wore an expensive oxblood cashmere dress and lynx stole on New Year's night when he proposed marriage and that she looked "like the Queen of Sheba did when she visited Solomon."[13] A printed card announcement of the Sunday-Thompson wedding on September 5, 1888, verifies that Billy's diligent pursuit of his quarry finally paid off.

Chapter 2
Caught on the Fly

For all of the positive benefits inherent in material culture interpretations, there are also drawbacks. First, not all artifacts survive the test of time. Typically weak interpretive areas in material culture include food, everyday clothing, work methods, social interaction habits, and language patterns. One author has gone so far as to assert that spoken language is actually a form of material culture, spoken words being air masses shaped by a speech apparatus according to culturally acquired rules.[1] Second, the depth of understanding that artifacts yield can sometimes be modest when compared to the complexity of analysis available through written accounts. In a historical context, emphasis is nearly always placed on the story first, with the artifact playing a supporting role. This technique of mixing written history with material culture is indeed powerful and, when properly managed, certainly the ideal means for conveying accurate interpretations of the past.

When material culture and written history clash, however, too often material evidence is ignored or, in the worst cases, purposefully eliminated in order to protect the interpretation from written or oral history. In the case of an unresolved conflict, it seems prudent that the barest, least complicated interpretation should be the one that is developed, even if that means calling into question a time-honored tradition. If an interpretive error is made due to this premise, it is made by erring on the side of caution.

When you finally reach home plate, the Great Umpire will call you either "Safe" or "Out." Which will it be, boys?
—BILLY SUNDAY (Lockerbie)

The Break

The young must have fun; if not at home, they will seek it in places they should not.—Billy Sunday Speaks!

Billy's return to the farm in Story County, Iowa, was not a smooth transition. After a short period working on his grandfather Cory's farm, he moved away from his family to the nearby town of Nevada, where he worked as an errand boy for a retired Union colonel, John Scott.[2] The Scotts took a personal interest in Billy and helped him continue his education at Nevada High School. He served as the school janitor to help pay for his tuition, but after so much hard work to earn a diploma, he skipped his graduation ceremony so that he could begin a new job with the Marshalltown Fire Brigade.[3]

The larger town of Marshalltown also had a highly respected semiprofessional baseball team, which Sunday was anxious to join. In 1882 the Marshalltown team won the state championship, and Sunday's performance was impressive enough to capture the attention of baseball legend Adrian "Cap" Anson of the Chicago White Stockings (later renamed the Chicago Cubs). Sunday jumped at the chance to try out for the pro team, quitting his job, spending his life savings of $6.00 on a new suit, and borrowing $4.50 for a train ticket and some spending money for the trip to Chicago. He arrived in the Windy City with $1.00 to his name.[4] Sunday not only made the Chicago team, he thrived as a professional baseball player. After five full seasons with the White Stockings, he was traded to the Pittsburgh Alleghenies (later renamed the Pittsburgh Pirates). His baseball career improved dramatically after the trade because he was more important to the Alleghenies as a regular starter than he had been to the White Stockings as a utility player. He played two and a half years with Pittsburgh before a midseason trade in 1890 to the Philadelphia Phillies in his final season before leaving baseball. During his eight-year professional baseball career, he made his mark stealing bases and was proclaimed by many the fastest man in baseball.[5] His skill at base stealing was so well known that after his final season, he was asked to assist in writing a how-to manual on the subject. While he exhibited his speed on the base paths and in the outfield, Sunday struggled somewhat at the plate, with a lifetime batting average of only .248. He made the most of that average by batting left-handed, putting himself one full stride closer to first base every time he entered the batter's box, even though he threw a baseball right-handed when fielding.

Relatively few artifacts from Sunday's professional baseball career have survived. A baseball, a fielder's glove, and a pair of cleats appear to be equipment from the appropriate time period of the 1880s (fig. 7). The small-handed webbing of the glove and the antiquated form of the cleats attest to a game played with more skill than technology or fancy equipment. But if the tools of the game were inferior by today's standards, the hearts of these early players certainly were not. An 1886 league champ-

FIGURE 7. *Clockwise from top: 1880s baseball and cleats, cut-glass crystal bat and ball presentation gift from employees of the Maryland Glass Corporation, 1891 Philadelphia contract, chromolithograph scorecards, 1927 umpire trophy, fielder's glove, Chicago Cubs season pass. Items courtesy of the Billy Sunday Historic Site Museum, Winona Lake, Indiana.*

ionship team photograph and three game scorecards from Sunday's first three years with the Chicago White Stockings confirm his position on the well-respected team. Interestingly, Billy Sunday is one of the few team members in the photograph without a mustache or facial hair of any kind (fig. 8). This departure from the norm suggests that even in 1886, prior to his conversion experience, he was his own person, different from the crowd around him, even if that crowd included world champion players. The three scorecards have color printed covers of players fielding fly balls, batting, and throwing to home. Chromolithography was still in its infancy in the 1880s, and these spectacularly colored scorecards prove the commitment of team owners to rouse the fervor of the game's fans. A state-of-the-art souvenir scorecard showed everyone that only the best would do for this game of baseball, and team owners were all too willing to do anything that might keep their fans excited. Professional baseball in the 1880s was still in a building process, but with the help of a few hundred of the nation's best athletes and a good deal of promotional money, the game was well on its way to becoming an American obsession.

The old Chicago White Stockings, national league winners in days before the Cubs and champions of the league in 1885 and 1886. Left to right (top row)— Billy Sunday, who played right field for this celebrated team; Dalrymple, left field; Williamson, shortstop; Jimmy Ryan, outfield, Flynn, pitcher, and Burns, third base. Lower row—Mike Kelly, catcher, Gore, center field; John Clarkson, pitcher; Moolic, catcher; Capt. Adrian C. Anson, first base; Pfeffer, second base; McCormick, pitcher, and Flint, catcher.

FIGURE 8. *Chicago White Stockings circa 1886. Billy Sunday is in the back row at the far left. Adrian "Cap" Anson is in center of the front row holding the bat. Image courtesy of the William and Helen Sunday Archives, Grace College, Winona Lake, Indiana.*

However, more telling than these items that hint of Sunday's involvement with the national pastime are six gifts that he received during his tenure in baseball. All six were given in 1888, the same year that Sunday married Nell Thompson and was traded from Chicago to Pittsburgh. The first gift was a presentation baseball bat made of numerous different inlaid hardwoods (fig. 9). A small brass shield plaque on the bat indicates that it was given to Sunday by "Friends in the Northwestern University," apparently for his services in coaching the college team that year. Sunday had been generously compensated for his coaching skills at Northwestern by being offered free tuition for course work at Evanston Academy, the college's prep school.[6] This presentation bat seems to be purely a token of esteem. Further, one is led to believe that the bat was a gift from the student-athletes to their coach rather than from the school, since it was inscribed "Friends in the Northwestern University." Typically, students are the ones "in" a university, whereas administrators or

FIGURE 9. *Clockwise from the upper left:* Thrift, Character *and* Duty *book set,* Moral Muscle and How to Use It, *presentation bat from Northwestern University, Sunday's travel Bible,* Out of My Bondage *history of the Pacific Garden Mission,* YMCA *medal,* Practical Elocution. *Items courtesy of the Billy Sunday Historic Site Museum, Winona Lake, Indiana.*

university representatives would be "of," "from," or "at" a university. One fact is certain — the bat was a gift and a sincere expression of gratitude. Sunday was well liked as an individual and served as a strong role model for youth.

The second and third gifts were wedding presents from the Chicago White Stockings to the new couple. An intricately carved oak parlor cabinet with its beveled mirror and cut fretwork doors exemplifies many of the stylistic ideals of the Victorian age and its emphasis on high ornamentation and the outward display of material wealth. An elaborately decorated Murphy bed was a perfectly appropriate gift for this young couple setting up housekeeping. His former White Stocking teammates gave these expensive items to the newlyweds shortly after Sunday had been traded to Pittsburgh.

The last three gifts were wedding presents from his Pittsburgh Alleghenies teammates and the team's administrators. An Ansonia brand mantle clock with two large medieval knights on either side of the clock case was presented as a gift from the Pittsburgh ball club's president on the field of play during an actual game shortly after Sunday's return from his honeymoon.[7] Ansonia clocks were among the most highly prized and expensive clocks of the day due to the ornately cast figures that typically adorned them. Sunday's new teammates also gave the couple a dining-room oak sideboard built in the American Empire style with large heavy carving, along with a small oak desk, which later became famous as the place of Billy's sermon writing and Nell's business correspondence. Like the parlor cabinet and Murphy bed from his former Chicago teammates, these gifts were made shortly after Sunday was traded. However, instead of a cast of old friends chipping in for the gifts, they were given to a couple barely known by the players who gave them.

Together, these six gifts provide a window into Sunday's personal relationships with peers like few other artifacts found in the home. None of these three groups were obligated to give Sunday anything more than a nominal gift. His work with the Northwestern team involved a coach-athlete relationship, which seldom produced lavish gifts. The Chicago White Stockings, while old friends of Sunday's, could have easily ignored their former teammate if they so desired — he was no longer on the team at the time of his wedding. Likewise, the Pittsburgh team could have easily justified neglecting a gift entirely, or most certainly could have given only a small token gift, since Sunday had just become a member of the team shortly before his wedding. Yet not only did all three groups give Billy Sunday gifts, they gave him and his bride extravagant gifts showing a tremendous outpouring of support and affection. Before he was a preacher, before he carried the banner for Prohibition, before he could claim to have spoken to more people in person than any man in history, there is material evidence demonstrating that Billy Sunday was extraordinarily well liked and admired by his peers.

Another remarkable artifact is Sunday's contract with Philadelphia for the 1891 season (fig. 7). This was the three-year contract that Sunday spoke of often in his sermons. Soon after signing it, he had a change of heart and asked for a release so that he might enter Christian work full-time. Philadelphia, however, at first denied his request. Sunday grudgingly agreed to play out his contract, then three months later in Nell's words, "the Lord didn't let him play it out," and Philadelphia mysteriously granted Sunday his release.[8] While the release from this contract resulted in a cut in pay from $2,800 per year in baseball to $1,000 per year at the Chicago YMCA, few things in his life had made Sunday happier than this release. It was the beginning of a road leading toward evangelism. Yet with his athletic style and flair for appealing to the common man and woman, it would always be evident that this preacher had once been a professional ballplayer.

These original baseball career items are bolstered by an additional twenty-one objects that relate to Sunday's ongoing relationship with the game long after his sports career had ended. Chicago Cubs 1906 and 1907 season passes, in which the "Sunday" name appears on the cover design as one of the past "famous league stars," are signed by Sunday and his oldest son, George (fig. 7). Framed, autographed photographs of the first three commissioners of major league baseball, Kenesaw Mountain Landis (who in 1935 served as a pallbearer at Sunday's funeral), A. B. "Happy" Chandler, and Ford Frick, as well as Hall of Fame pitcher Walter Johnson, adorned the walls of Sunday's study. Hidden corners of the home yield newer baseballs, a more recent fielder's glove, a catcher's mitt and gear, a uniform Sunday wore during exhibition games in the 1910s and 1920s, and numerous photographs of him playing with the likes of Douglas Fairbanks, Homer Rodeheaver, and other notables at those games. Presentation gifts, such as a bronze trophy given as a gift to Sunday for umpiring a game during the 1927 revival in Aurora, Illinois, kept his image close to the sport (fig. 7). These artifacts all play upon Sunday's baseball career in much the same way he did in his own sermons, as a type of marketing hook. The Baseball Evangelist was a popular preacher at the top of his new game, and he took full advantage of his historic association with the national pastime.

Getting Religion

For every daredevil there should be a daresaint.
—Billy Sunday Speaks!

Historians still debate whether Billy Sunday was living the rough-and-rowdy lifestyle expected of anyone playing professional baseball in the 1880s. In those early baseball days, the typical ballplayer drank heavily and stayed out until odd hours of the night carousing with women of questionable virtue. Most accounts reflect that Sunday was not immune to these vices, but at the same time he never wholeheartedly plunged into this carefree lifestyle. While written records conflict on the actual year of his conversion (1885, 1886, or 1887), all descriptions contain certain consistencies.[9] One day while out with his ballplayer buddies in a somewhat inebriated state of consciousness, Sunday came in contact with members of the Pacific Garden Mission. This traveling caravan played music and held brief sermons right in the heart of Chicago's saloon district in an effort to get a few individuals to follow them back to the mission. The music stirred old feelings of his youth, where Sunday listened for hours to his mother singing hymns as she worked at her chores. Sunday got up, turned to his teammates, and said, "I'm through. We've come to a parting of the ways."[10] He went straight to the mission that afternoon for more songs and sermons and returned there several times the following week, until one night he finally decided that it was time to answer the altar call and formally declare that he was a reborn Christian. Sunday later reflected on that night as the watershed event of his life.[11] This is the story the written histories give of Billy Sunday's conversion — an emotional, divinely inspired turnaround for a twenty-three-year-old man headed down a dark path of sin.

Sunday probably experienced these events. However, he most certainly had been searching quite some time for direction before his miraculous conversion. He spoke many times over the course of his preaching career of a foot race he ran in St. Louis against Arlie Latham of the St. Louis Browns and the mental anguish this race caused him. While Sunday himself did not wager any money on the race, his manager, Cap Anson, had personally put up $1,000, and a total of $75,000 was riding on the outcome of the race.[12] Sunday had a change of heart after the wagering began and asked Anson to let him out of the arrangement, but Anson refused, and Sunday went on to run the race. He won, but he claimed that he felt an evil burden upon his soul for participating in this high stakes race. One artifact may directly reflect his apprehension and soul-searching during this time. At about the same time as the race, he purchased his first Bible — not a fancy one to impress those who would see it but a simple, small travel Bible from a secondhand bookstore in St. Louis (fig. 9). There is a high probability that he purchased this Bible prior to his conversion episode, and perhaps he obtained it immediately before or after the foot race. Of course, a travel Bible made a good deal of sense for a ballplayer living out of a suitcase. Knowing the lifestyle of his peers, it was also easier to hide from potentially taunting eyes. This little book, unceremoniously found in a heap of objects in a closet of the home, speaks volumes on the state of Sunday's mind at the time of the Pacific Garden Mission experience.

The travel Bible provides potent material evidence that there may not have been a lightning bolt sending a potential inhabitant of hell into an about-face. Instead, here was a man who had already acknowledged his own unfulfilled state and was searching for answers. The Bible contains a few reader's marks and notes, and it does appear to have been read through several times. Whether all of these usage hallmarks were made by Sunday or by the book's previous owner, one will never know, but it seems reasonable to presume that Sunday would not go out of his way to purchase a Bible convenient in size and shape for his travels and then not read it. He remarked years later in an authorized biography that this Bible only cost him thirty-five cents in 1886, but in 1914 he would not take $3,500 for it.[13] Perhaps it is not so surprising that the official date of Sunday's conversion has been lost to history through conflicting documentary accounts, as one recent biographer put it.[14] Sunday could not recall the exact date of this monumental change in his life possibly because the change may have been well under way before he had even heard of the Pacific Garden Mission.

Nonetheless, the Pacific Garden Mission remained in Billy Sunday's life and legacy. A framed photograph of the interior of the mission at Easter services in 1896 hung on the wall of his study (fig. 10). Sunday donated his entire personal compensation of $58,000 from the 1918 nine-week-long Chicago revival to the organization so that the mission might purchase its first property and establish a permanent endowment.[15] Years after Sunday's death, the Pacific Garden Mission built an addition dubbed the Billy Sunday Chapel, to which Nell Sunday donated a large oil portrait of Billy, which traditionally hung in the living room at the Sunday home.[16] Nell possessed ten copies of *Out of My Bondage: Excerpts from a Doorway to Heaven*, a small booklet published in 1940 by the Pacific Garden Mission chronicling the history and success of that organization (fig. 9). Of course, the first chapter of the booklet succinctly outlines the success of its most famous convert, Billy Sunday. Shortly before she died, Nell also received a copy of the 1955 publication *Not the Righteous!* by the famous Pacific Garden Mission radio broadcaster Jack Odell.

Sunday's Pacific Garden Mission conversion marked a turning point in his life from which he never backtracked. Almost immediately after the conversion, he changed his behavior patterns off the field and began spending free time at Chicago's YMCA in a Bible study class. When Sunday began to take rhetoric course work at Evanston Academy in the 1887–1888 off-season, J. W. Shoemaker's *Practical Elocution* was a likely

FIGURE 10. *Easter celebration at the Pacific Garden Mission in 1896. Image courtesy of the William and Helen Sunday Archives, Grace College, Winona Lake, Indiana.*

a textbook (fig. 9). While still a player, he was sought after by many in the church community, especially the YMCA organizations in towns where he was playing, to give inspirational speeches and encourage young men to follow Christ. John H. Elliot's *Suggestive Teaching Outlines for Workers Training Classes* provides insights into some of the messages that Sunday probably shared during those first public-speaking engagements. He played baseball for another four seasons after his conversion to Christianity, but during this time he certainly didn't live the common ballplayer's lifestyle.

Young Man!

If you live wrong, you can't die right.
—The Real Billy Sunday *(Brown)*

Surprisingly, just when his dollar value as a baseball player reached its peak, Billy Sunday decided to leave the game and dedicate his life's work to serving his God. For the 1891 season, two teams, Philadelphia and Cincinnati, offered him lucrative contracts. The Philadelphia contract was for $400 a month for three years, while the Cincinnati contract was $500 per month for one year. Considering that the average income of a factory worker was $380 for an entire year, these seven-month seasonal contract offers were obviously attractive. They gave Sunday the means to support his wife, a new baby daughter, his mother, and his oldest brother, Albert, who had become an invalid.[17] Instead of cashing in, however, he decided to leave baseball for good and take a full-time position with the YMCA at $83.33 per month.[18]

Artifacts from this time period foreshadow the career yet to come for Sunday. Josiah Strong's *Our Country: Its Possible Future and Its Present Crisis* hardly seems like casual reading material for a ballplayer, but in 1887 Sunday was given this book, which dealt with weighty social issues. Similarly, two Christian worker training books by Samuel Smiles entitled *Duty* and *Character* lead one to believe that Sunday had been considering life after baseball for more than a year prior to actually requesting his release in 1890 (fig. 9). J. B. McClure's *Moody's Anecdotes & Illustrations* was probably used during his Bible-study courses at the YMCA and likely provided the conservative religious foundations on which Sunday would later help to build the Fundamentalist movement. An application book for membership in the Chicago YMCA dating from the 1880s, like the artifacts from the Pacific Garden Mission, points toward the beginning of Sunday's long relationship with that Christian organization.

Four books in Sunday's possession highlight the two and a half years he spent working for the Chicago YMCA. Sunday inscribed his signature and "Feby, -91 Chicago, Ill. YMCA Training School" inside the cover of *Moral Muscle and How to Use It* by Frederick A. Atkins (fig. 9). This text may well have been one of the first items handed to him as he began formal training for his employment at the "Y." The title would remain an accurate platitude of Sunday's approach to faith, salvation, and deviant social behavior throughout his preaching career, as he always linked moral strength to physical prowess. *First Battles and How to Fight Them*, also by Frederick A. Atkins, and *To the Work* by Dwight L. Moody are instructive texts for the Christian worker. Both books endorse aggressive evangelism as the most effective means to achieving God's will. Perhaps most telling of Sunday's personal life during this period is Samuel Smile's *Thrift* (fig. 9). The book contains information valuable to someone in

FIGURE 11. *Nell Sunday is holding her second child, George, in a shabby photography studio in 1892. The life of want and spareness during Billy's YMCA days is plainly evident in the less than ideal surroundings of this unnamed studio and the blank gaze on Nell's face. Image courtesy of the William and Helen Sunday Archives, Grace College, Winona Lake, Indiana.*

Sunday's shoes, who had just left a very lucrative occupation in exchange for the meager income offered through Christian work at the Chicago YMCA (fig. 11). A decade later Sunday came into the possession of *Studies for Personal Workers*, published by the International Committee of YMCA, and *The Religious Condition of Young Men* by James F. Oates, published by the Central Department YMCA of Chicago. In 1905 he was presented with a solid gold medal for service with the "Y." The organization's motto — "Mind, Spirit, Body"—on the medal still resonates with the principles of mental, spiritual, and physical cleanliness that Sunday espoused.

Chapter 3
Revival Machine

Much of the evidence about Billy Sunday's life that exists as material culture takes the form of books in the Sunday library. Of course, recorded accounts are artifacts in their own right, and such artifacts exist in a variety of forms. Paper items containing written or visual documentation such as ticket stubs, billing receipts, contracts, photographs, and drawings are all considered unbiased artifacts in that their existence is not an interpretation of a past event but instead a witness to it. However, within the sphere of material culture studies, it is generally accepted that the written and oral accounts of historic figures or events contained in material collections are excluded from analysis due to possible author bios. On the other hand, artifacts that contain written accounts, such as books, magazines, and correspondence, are considered valid material culture components because such items represent the interests and experiences of the objects' owner. In a material culture study, these items are interpreted as examples of subject matter and writers, rather than reference resources. This is a subtle point that separates the field of history from that of material culture studies, but it is a point well worth making, since written documents will be used significantly in this work.

Learning a New Game

*I don't know any more about theology than a jack-rabbit
does about ping-pong, but I'm on the way to glory.*
—Billy Sunday: The Man and His Message *(Ellis)*

From 1891 to 1896 Billy Sunday took on the role of an evangelical apprentice. During his two and a half years at the Chicago YMCA, he visited the homes of the poor, learned firsthand how alcohol could destroy lives, and became convinced that salvation through Jesus Christ was the only answer for society's ills.[1] The well-known evangelist J. Wilbur Chapman knew of Billy Sunday's baseball fame when, in 1894, he found him at the YMCA. Chapman offered Sunday the position of advance man for his revival circuit. As an advance man, Sunday was responsible for traveling to cities and towns days ahead of Chapman, making arrangements for venues, organizing local church support, selling Bibles, and leading a few worship services until Chapman's arrival. Once the Reverend Chapman arrived, Sunday was off to the next city to do it all over again. While the travel was difficult, Chapman paid him significantly better than the YMCA, and being on the road gave Sunday a renewed sense of excitement that he had dearly missed since leaving baseball. More important, working for Chapman gave Sunday a hands-on course in how to run an evangelistic campaign. During his two years of advance work for Chapman, he learned much about preaching, sermon writing, and the stylistic flair necessary for keeping an audience's attention. It was also during this period that Sunday began to wear only the finest clothing while in public in order to impress those whom he met.

As an advance man setting up the details of Chapman's revivals, Sunday often spent much time on his own away from both his family and his employer. George D. Herron's *The Larger Christ*, given to Sunday in 1894, would have been of great use to the young assistant (fig. 12). In addition, the Sundays had two nicely framed photographs of their old friend Rev. Chapman hanging in their home. While no other artifact directly related to Sunday's involvement with Chapman is to be found, the setting of the Sundays' home, the community of Winona Lake, is itself a gigantic material manifestation of Chapman's impact on Sunday. Chapman was one of the early founders of Winona Lake as a center for religious conferences and a Chautauqua site in the mid 1890s, and he held the position of Winona Lake Bible Conference director for many years.[2] Chapman encouraged Sunday to bring his young family to Winona Lake and participate in the lectures. Wanting to please his boss, Sunday gladly complied. Without Chapman's influence, it is questionable whether Billy Sunday would have chosen Winona Lake as a place to spend vacations and eventually call home. Years after Sunday's apprenticeship had ended with Chapman, his mentor gave him a copy of his book, *From Life to Life* (fig. 12).

In December 1895 Chapman grew tired of the traveling circuit and decided to take a pastoral post at Bethany Presbyterian Church in Philadelphia.[3] This change suddenly left Sunday without a job. But only days after learning of his new state of unemployment, he received a telegram from three preachers in Garner, Iowa, who wanted him to lead

FIGURE 12. *Clockwise from the upper left:* The Iconoclast; *soapstone lighthouse; bronze of Jesus entering Jerusalem; framed photograph of J. Wilbur Chapman;* The Larger Christ; Men, Monkeys and Missing Links; From Life to Life; The Proof of God. *Items courtesy of the Billy Sunday Historic Site Museum, Winona Lake, Indiana.*

a week-long revival for them. He accepted their offer, delivered 268 converts in eight days, and began a storied evangelistic career.[4] Playing off his prior fame as a baseball player, Sunday's reputation for fiery sermons grew regionally throughout Iowa and other midwestern states where he led tent revivals (fig. 13). Just as Chapman had done, Sunday hired an advance man to organize details of a town's revival. When Sunday arrived in town, the two men, along with local volunteers, would raise a rented circus-style tent. During these early years of his preaching, Sunday was well liked by all he met because of his hands-on, low-brow approach to the manual labor that needed to be accomplished. Sunday enjoyed the social aspects of physical labor throughout his life, and it is a direct reflection of his ability to relate to the common working person (fig. 14). As one resident of Winona Lake put it: "He didn't know a stranger. You'd see him all the time in the park dressed in dirty old clothes, stabbing trash with a stick to keep the place looking nice."[5]

During the early period of Sunday's preaching career, he developed a theological approach consistent with the movement that later became

SCORING RUNS OFF SATAN'S DELIVERY.

William A. Sunday, the Old League Ballplayer, in the Evangelistic Field.

W. A. SUNDAY.　　　　　**FRENCH E. OLIVER.**

When Billy Sunday wore the uniform of a ballplayer in the League he was fleet of foot and ranked among the best rungetters in that organization. His retirement from the diamond was voluntary. He refused an offer from the Cincinnati Club, and entered the field as an evangelist. For three weeks past Sunday has figured in one of the most remarkable revivals in the religious history of Indiana. Assisted by French E. Oliver he has stirred Salem as it was never before stirred. "The Devil's Boomerangs Up To Date" was the title of one of his best addresses. When the time came for parting the scenes at the depot were remarkable. There were prayers and songs in open air, followed by cheers for the young men who had created so much enthusiasm for the Gospel cause.

FIGURE 13. *This 1897 newspaper announcement capitalizes heavily on Sunday's baseball career. French Oliver went on to become an outspoken evangelist in his own right after his experience with Sunday. Image courtesy of the William and Helen Sunday Archives, Grace College, Winona Lake, Indiana.*

FIGURE 14. *Billy Sunday cleaning up the front yard at the Mount Hood bungalow in Winona Lake. Image courtesy of the William and Helen Sunday Archives, Grace College, Winona Lake, Indiana.*

known as Fundamentalism — literal biblical interpretation, a premillennial second coming of Christ, and conservative stances on scientific knowledge, amusements, and social reform. One of the most prevalent criticisms hurled at Sunday was that he was shallow, poorly educated, and overly simplistic in his theology due to his own limited mental faculties. The size and breadth of his library, as well as the numerous handwritten notes and reader's marks found in a substantial proportion of the books, clearly refute this interpretation. Before there existed a defined preaching classification of Fundamentalist, Billy Sunday was one. This new "old-time religion" of Fundamentalism, a militantly antimodernist Protestant evangelicalism, grew to prominence largely as a reaction against twentieth-century secularism or liberalist forms of Christianity such as the Social Gospel.[6] Sunday believed that the best way to beat this modernist onslaught was to use science, the modernists' strongest tool, against them. In *The Proof of God* by Harold Begbie, Sunday underscores whole sections of text that he apparently was considering using in some context for his own sermons (fig. 12). *Science: The False Messiah* by C. E. Ayres and Howard A. Kelly's *A Scientific Man and the Bible* were other attempts to prove God's existence by using methods of science, relying heavily on the Bible as a primary documentary source and testimonials of modern scientists who professed their absolute faith in God. Armed with his own version of scientific proof, Sunday was prepared to take on any comers who dared to claim that Jesus was anything less than the son of God.

Sunday railed against Charles Darwin's notion of biological evolution with ample help from A. Wilford Hall's *The Problem of Human Life* and four booklets by Arthur I. Brown — *Men, Monkeys and Missing Links* (fig. 12); *Evolution and Blood-Precipitation Test; Was Darwin Right?;* and *Evolution and the Bible.* These texts gave Sunday the ammunition that he needed to undercut scientific authority and establish his own empirical evidence disputing the validity of evolution. On the topic of social evolution, Sunday relied heavily on Joseph Husslein's *Evolution and Social Progress,* and he cut deep into the heart of the physical sciences with the classic text *The Religion of Geology and Its Connected Sciences* by Edward Hitchcock.

Elements of Sunday's message, such as evolution, his clear disdain toward the influx of eastern European immigrants, and his inconsistent position in dealing with the American black population, revealed an overlapping with views espoused by radical creationists and the Ku Klux

Klan. During the evening service of May 14, 1922, of his revival in Richmond, Indiana, twelve members of the Klan dressed in full regalia entered shortly after Sunday began his sermon and approached the platform to the great anxiety of the crowd in attendance.[7] They handed him a letter and check for $50 to support the Winona Lake religious school, the organization that was to receive the night's offerings. After the Klansmen retreated from the tabernacle, Homer Rodeheaver publicly read the letter, which thanked Sunday for his positive influence upon the city of Richmond and espoused the Klan's endorsement of Christian values and white supremacy. Sunday proclaimed to the crowd that he was not a member of the Ku Klux Klan, but then he made light of the event by admitting he was relieved that they came to give him something instead of taking him away, and he thankfully accepted their check to the amusement of the audience. At the concluding day of his 1924 revival in Charlotte, North Carolina, the Klan presented him with a check for $225, to which he remarked, "I don't know why we should not have an organization that excludes Catholics and Jews if the Catholics have organizations which exclude Protestants and the Jews have organizations of the same type."[8] This statement was in marked contrast to Sunday's typical open-door policy toward all Judeo-Christian groups, for less than a decade earlier, Sunday met personally with Cardinal James Gibbons of the Catholic Church of Baltimore in an air of cooperation and friendship ensuring the ecumenical success of that city's revival.[9] This shift of attitude in the 1920s is perhaps a sign that Sunday played more to the appeal of the local crowd than the image projected in his public persona. The next year during his campaign in Winston-Salem, North Carolina, the local chapter of the Klan took out a half-page ad in the *Winston-Salem Journal* endorsing Sunday's revival on the very first day that he was to offer a "colored only" meeting (fig. 15). The conspicuous nature of the advertisement's timing was an unmistakable attempt at intimidation, yet Sunday failed to comment on the imposing gesture, instead offering a passive stance of neutrality, which he often employed on the issue of race relations. His inability to publicly distance himself from groups like the Klan contributed significantly to his dwindling support in the 1920s.

When it came to the fields of science and history, Billy Sunday knew he was up against formidable enemies with mountains of empirical evidence, so he did what any good scientist or historian would do — he researched. Sunday studied these fields from the inside out, purchasing books meant to prove scientific theories or historical interpretations,

FIGURE 15. *Ku Klux Klan advertisement in the* Winston-Salem Journal *endorsing Billy Sunday during this 1925 revival in North Carolina. Image courtesy of the* Winston-Salem Journal, *Winston-Salem, North Carolina.*

then searching for holes in the authors' arguments. Just for reference purposes, he owned two ten-volume sets of Edgar Sanderson's *The World's History and Its Makers*, a four-volume set of *The People's Natural History Series*, four volumes of the demographic text *The World Survey Series*, the twelve-volume 1913 edition of *Nelson's Perpetual Loose-Leaf Encyclopedia*, and the 1907 version of *A Complete Atlas of the World*. Perhaps his most surprising reference tool is an unabridged twelve-volume set of *The Works of Brann: The Iconoclast*, self-published by William Cowper Brann in 1919 (fig. 12). In the view of many conservative Christians, Brann was perhaps the most outspoken heretic of the New World, brazenly combating all religions as mere superstition in his Texas periodical, the *Iconoclast*. Sunday not only owned his own copy of Brann's work, he used it thoroughly, underlining text and making notes on how he would combat this foe.

Sunday's critics had grown more bold in the 1920s. Several short books and leaflets were published denouncing Sunday's doctrine as materialistic and plagiarized. One book, *Billy Sunday U-N-M-A-S-K-E-D*, blasted Sunday for perverting Scripture. The book reprinted his sermon transcripts next to the actual biblical quotations that he referenced. Sunday's use of slang terminology was of particular concern, even though he always maintained that he used slang to keep the message close to the common man and woman. The book also reprinted Sunday's much acclaimed Decoration Day address and a virtually identical Decoration Day speech from 1882 by noted agnostic Robert Ingersoll.[10] The obvious plagiarism of Ingersoll proved very damaging since Sunday often recounted with great pride an incident during his YMCA days when he led a public protest of an Ingersoll lecture series in Chicago, and he regularly listed "Atheist Bob" as one of the modernists surely to be found in hell.[11] Deep in the recesses of a bookcase in the Sunday library rests an 1899 copy of *Ingersollia: Gems of Thought from the Lectures, Speeches and Conversations of the Late Col. Robert G. Ingersoll* by Thomas W. Hanford. It contains pages of underlined text and notes Sunday presumably made in developing sermons. The presence of this book and the wholesale underlining of text in many volumes in Sunday's library provide material evidence to strengthen the critics' claims of plagiarism. While it was common practice for preachers to lift text from others' works and use it in sermons without proper citation, in the case of Billy Sunday, he would publish his sermons in pamphlet form for sale in his tabernacles. Thus the charge of plagiarism bore considerable weight. One antagonistic Sunday biographer estimated that 75 percent of his sermons were borrowed from others' works.[12] Plagiarism aside, the mere possession of *Ingersollia* and the *Iconoclast* would have been enough to raise the eyebrows of any decent Christian. For Sunday not only to keep a bound set on public display but also to use the controversial texts for sermon development could only mean that he did indeed dig deeply into the thoughts and backgrounds of his opponents in much the same way academic scholars fully research the viewpoints of their adversaries.

Billy Sunday's conservative philosophy took root quickly in a society inundated by radical change. Technological changes such as indoor plumbing, electrical appliances, telephones, radios, and automobiles, as well as social changes involving urban sprawl, heavy industrialization, political unrest, and the flight of youth from the farm, created an unprecedented air of instability. Sunday's message struck a chord with a nation fearful of these changes. Moreover, he offered specific answers to alleviate the public's fears. Demographically, the largest issues were foreign immigration and the flight of rural youth from the farm to the city. To be an American, to Billy Sunday, meant the revocation of allegiance to one's ethnic heritage, and he believed that the same foreign-born immigrant groups that opposed temperance also were responsible for labor unrest, radical views of government, and plots to undermine America. "I believe the ten million aliens in this country who have been content to seek fortune under the protecting folds [of the] Stars and Stripes, but who refused to be assimilated should be dug up — to the last man and made to kiss the American flag or go back to lands from which [they] came," exclaimed Sunday in one sermon.[13] The atheism associated with the Bolsheviks in Russia presented another manifestation of Satan, which he fought publicly. Sunday played on the latent fears of a nation in transition, a transition that simultaneously offered both hope and exploitation for millions of foreign immigrants. Would these immigrants become upstanding American citizens, or would they drag the United States into Europe's moral and political mess? More and more, Billy Sunday began to equate anything foreign with an innate defect that could only be overcome through Jesus Christ and, perhaps, capitalism.

On the plight of the farmer, whom he always held in the highest regard due to his own rural upbringing, Sunday came down on the side of the new majority, urban Americans. The 1920 census revealed for the first time in the nation's history that more citizens lived in cities than on farms. Sunday himself was one of those converts, and while he looked back nostalgically on his days in Iowa, he most certainly did not forget the hard, painful lifestyle that the farm required. His oldest friends were on the farm, but he spent more time with his new friends in the city. His close circle of supporters included the industrial and retailing barons of the day: John D. Rockefeller Jr., John M. Studebaker, H. J. Heinz, Henry Leland, S. S. Kresge, and John Wanamaker. He believed that the ongoing economic transformation that had made America rich was in some way a sign from God that industrial, urban America was on the right track if, and only if, those in the city would cleanse themselves and give their hearts to Jesus Christ. That was Sunday's job.

Sunday exploited to his best advantage these changes in technology and society, which for many created apprehension and fear. He marveled at modern conveniences such as the automobile, and in 1910 he took an airplane ride over Winona Lake with famous aviator Glenn H. Curtiss.[14] Ironically, he used the tools of the modern age, such as planes, trains, and automobiles, to take him to the revivals where he would denounce the societal ills of the same modern age, seeking a return to Victorian moral values. One of the social matters with which Sunday took issue was that of labor reform. He supported the common laborer, but he looked to the conscience and soul of the business owner as the means to improve the worker's lot in life. For this reason, Sunday often denounced labor strikes, comparing them to treason in the military. The fact that his revivals were frequently sponsored by the wealthy industrialists of a city often cast a shadow of doubt on Sunday's true allegiance. In 1915 George Creel wrote a scathing article, "Salvation Circus: An Estimate of Billy Sunday," in *Harper's Weekly*, exposing some of Sunday's connections to big business and the "coincidental" appearance of Sunday campaigns in districts with potential labor unrest (fig. 16). Many of Sunday's critics argued that he offered no real solutions to societal problems, just more revivalism in a circus-style atmosphere.[15]

Perhaps this dichotomy in Sunday's approach is best reflected in two facets of the family's possessions. First, the bungalow architecture of the home itself is a complex mix of the romanticized view of the self-reliant early American craftsman ideal and the modern conveniences of the twentieth-century home. A full analysis of what the bungalow meant in American culture appears later in this work, but it is worth noting here that this home is a perfect example of Sunday's looking to the past in order to find answers for the present. Second, one of the biggest surprises from a material culture standpoint is the paucity of overtly religious artifacts outside of the library collection. One would naturally expect Billy Sunday's home to be virtually brimming over with religious iconography, but such is not the case. The most striking artifact of this nature is a large bronze and silver statue of Jesus entering Jerusalem on a donkey (fig. 12). This figure, created by Alfred Nygard and cast at the Roman Bronze Works in New York, is an outstanding example of early-twentieth-century bronze sculpture. Unfortunately, and almost alarmingly, there is no record of how or when the Sundays came into possession of such a highly prized piece of American art. Nell Sunday took great pains to document the origins of most items in the home, and yet this prime example of an explicitly religious subject somehow fell through the cracks.

Very few images of Jesus Christ adorn the home. One such object, which hangs in the gallery hall, is the engraved print entitled *The Friend of the Lowly*. A small color print in a hand-carved, arched frame depicting Christ on the cross at Calvary as well as a color-tinted drawing of Jesus were both found on the walls of the butler's pantry. A framed black-and-white photograph of the ruins at Jamestown Church, Virginia, and a large oil painting of Mission San Diego del Alcala in California by G. Heffland Bigelow provide a cursory illustration of church history in the

FIGURE 16. *Cover of* Harper's Weekly *containing the feature article by George Creel, "Salvation Circus: An Estimate of Billy Sunday." Image courtesy of the William and Helen Sunday Archives, Grace College, Winona Lake, Indiana.*

New World. A carved soapstone lighthouse, complete with a small Christmas-style lightbulb inside to illuminate the entire figure, would have made a handy night-light or interesting conversation piece (fig. 12). Of course, the lighthouse has long been used as a Christian icon symbolizing safety and salvation through knowledge, but one must wonder in this case if this small lighthouse was not casting a beacon in search of more signs of religious heritage.

The Master's Showman

They tell me a revival is only temporary; so is a bath, but it does you good.
—Twenty Years with Billy Sunday *(Rodeheaver)*

Sunday's popularity grew slowly during his first years of preaching; he was by no means an overnight success. In order to expand his audience base in his early preaching days, he became a regular speaker on the Chautauqua circuit. Begun in 1874 in Chautauqua, New York, these gatherings exposed the public to the notion of self-improvement through education, recreation, and often a healthy dose of Christian evangelism. Chautauquas were organized throughout the country, and if a speaker's name was widely known, he or she could do well simply by traveling from one Chautauqua to the next, delivering lectures or inspirational messages. Sunday's message was usually on temperance, and through the Chautauqua circuit, he became a national leader of the cause.[16] One of the largest Chautauqua conferences was held every year in Winona Lake.

The typical Billy Sunday revival program followed a predictable format. A long program of gospel music, directed by Homer Rodeheaver, always opened the meeting. During the music, Sunday discreetly walked up an aisle to the stage, usually placed in the center of the tabernacle so that the audience encircling him would be as close as possible.[17] When he felt the time was right, which varied according to the behavior of the audience, he would begin. Sunday was very particular about silence. If the crowd chattered, he would stare them down. Many times before beginning his sermon, Rodeheaver instructed the crowd for a few moments on techniques for muffling coughs and sneezes in order to maintain silence.[18] Of course, infants were expressly forbidden within the sanctuary of the tabernacle, and for this reason many of his tabernacles were equipped with nurseries. The sawdust flooring was yet another means of dampening the noise from shuffling feet. Ubiquitous and

FIGURE 17. *The interior of the Boston tabernacle in 1916 clearly shows the famous sawdust-covered aisle. Image courtesy of the William and Helen Sunday Archives, Grace College, Winona Lake, Indiana.*

inexpensive, the sawdust covering the aisles served more than just a utilitarian function. First connected with Sunday in his 1900s revivals in Washington State and Oregon, the idea of a sawdust trail came from the timber industry. Loggers used sawdust to mark their way into uncut timber forests and then find their way back to camp. The sawdust trail at a Billy Sunday revival took on a spiritual meaning of coming out of the darkness and back into light, comfort, and home.[19] The term "hitting the sawdust trail" became synonymous with the converts who came forward at Sunday's invitation to shake his hand and accept Christ as their personal savior (fig. 17) (appendix B).

During the sermon, Sunday spoke from behind the pulpit, in front of the pulpit, and his favorite place, on top of the pulpit. His original

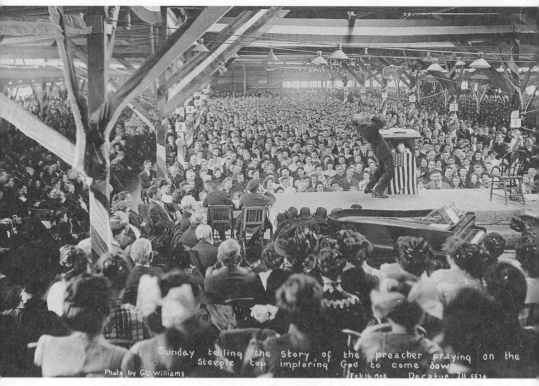

FIGURE 18. *Billy Sunday captivates his audience in 1908 at the Decatur, Illinois, revival. Image courtesy of the William and Helen Sunday Archives, Grace College, Winona Lake, Indiana.*

sermon notes in loose-leaf binders show the oversize typeface and all-caps printing style that he used for his handwritten notes so that he could easily view the text as he sprinted past the pulpit. He smashed his fists on the top and sides of the pulpit, attempting to break off a small piece, if he was lucky, for dramatic effect (fig. 18). He leaped from pulpit to piano, ran up and down the aisles, slid on the stage as if he were sliding into home plate, and often smashed an ordinary chair to bits. He performed these physical feats to drive home his points of theological fundamentalism and simultaneously keep his audience spellbound. Typically during the course of a revival, he delivered two sermons per day, Tuesday through Friday, and three sermons per day on Saturday and Sunday. His revivals were sometimes as short as two weeks but, more often, five to seven weeks in length. Although he always remained in superb physical condition, it is understandable that he required a rubdown after every sermon.[20] Physical health, particularly weight, seemed to be an obsession with Sunday, since three bathroom scales are found in the home, one of which is an elaborate doctor's scale to give precise measurements.

During the years 1908 to 1920 Billy Sunday's popularity skyrocketed. He was the subject of more than sixty articles in popular magazines such as *Collier's, Ladies Home Journal,* and *Harper's Weekly,* and it seemed that everywhere he went, there was a photographer ready to take his picture (fig. 19). In 1914 Sunday ranked eighth on the "Greatest Man in America" list in *American Magazine.*[21] Scores of newborn boys were named "Billy Sunday" in his honor, and in Fulton County, Illinois, a recipe for "Billy Sunday Pudding" was formulated by local residents. The pudding was designed to bake in the oven during his sermon and be ready when the family came home from the meeting.[22] He even worked his way into popular literature in 1916 when Indiana author Theodore Dreiser commented at length (disapprovingly) on Sunday's impact on the nation's landscape in *A Hoosier Holiday.*[23] Later, in 1927, a veritable riot broke out over Sinclair Lewis's novel *Elmer Gantry,* which depicts a fraudulent preacher manipulating the masses with promises of heaven in exchange for heavy offerings. The character of Elmer Gantry was regularly drunk while he preached abstinence, womanized while he warned of eternal damnation, and plagiarized from agnostics, including Robert Ingersoll. Some of the similarities to Sunday's life were so obvious that Lewis included the statement "No character in this book is the portrait of any actual person" inside the front cover just to avoid any possible lawsuit.[24] Sunday himself entered into the fray by vehemently denouncing the book's intentions.

During his thirty-nine years of evangelism, Sunday held 548 documented revivals or isolated speaking appearances in forty American states and one Canadian province (see appendix A), and he preached to more than 100 million people, the vast majority between the years 1908 and 1920.[25] Shortly before his death in 1935, Sunday estimated for *Ladies' Home Journal* that he had delivered nearly 20,000 sermons over the course of his lifetime, yielding an average of 42 sermons per month since he began his preaching career in 1896. Better records that were kept of his sawdust trail hitters, people who came forward to shake his hand, indicate that Sunday converted or reaffirmed the faith of 870,075 people (see appendix B).[26] In terms of his first career, that's less than a

FIGURE 19. *Billy decides to become the photographer while Nell is his willing subject in 1916. Team member Virginia Asher holds camera in center while Albert Peterson is at the far right behind Nell. Image courtesy of the William and Helen Sunday Archives, Grace College, Winona Lake, Indiana.*

.009 batting average. Does this mean that more than 99 percent of the people who saw him preach were not moved enough by a divine spirit to proclaim their faith? Hardly. Those who were comfortable with their personal relationship with God and did not want to publicly display it did not come forward. Nonetheless, Billy Sunday revivals were phenomenal events, and many attended as mere spectators. The Sunday "show" was a well-crafted arrangement meant not only to deliver the word of God but also to entertain, much in the same fashion as a traveling circus or vaudeville act.[27] Before the days of radio, movies, and television, modern Americans of the twentieth century actively sought out new forms of entertainment, and Billy Sunday promised to provide the greatest show ever seen — a chance to win salvation or watch while others were saved (fig. 20). Always wanting to make his campaigns seem bigger than life, for a 1907 revival in Knoxville, Iowa, he even enlisted the help of a former Barnum and Bailey "giant" to serve as chief usher.[28]

One manner of assessing Sunday's true impact on the public's emotions is to measure the gifts that he and Nell received during his evangelistic career. Many of the gifts given to the Sundays capitalized on his former career as a baseball player in the same manner that Sunday himself did in his sermons. Employees of the Maryland Glass Corporation in Baltimore presented him with a cut-glass crystal bat and baseball during his campaign there in 1916 (fig. 7). The ball carries the trademark "The Gospel of Jesus Christ" in place of the standard Spalding trademark. In similar fashion, the Sterling Engine Company of Buffalo, New York, gave him an oversized wooden baseball bearing the inscription "Bawl out the sinners 'Billy' keep on knocking 'em out" (fig. 21). A colorized photograph of a young boy wearing catcher's gear with the caption "Put it over Bill" was likely a gift from an adoring fan during the Pittsburgh campaign of 1913. Two more presentation bats, one with the inscription "The Wagon Tongue," symbolically melding Sunday's baseball career with his fight against alcohol, cap off the baseball theme gifts.

Some of the most striking gifts the Sundays received were utilitarian decorative art pieces. A pair of art glass vases and matching lamp, Weller and Rookwood art pottery, and numerous examples of cut-glass vessels bear testimony to the cutting-edge tastes of the Sundays' personal friends. The employees of the Steubenville Pottery Company took a page from the famous archaeologist Howard Carter's notebook in producing a neo-Egyptian cocoa set for the Sundays (fig. 21). The pitcher is monogrammed in gold leaf with "William A. Sunday" on the side so that there was no mistaking this American pharaoh. The city of Richmond, Indiana, presented the Sundays with a large landscape painting by the city's famous resident John Elwood Bundy, one of the best-known artists of the Hoosier Impressionist school during the early twentieth century. The grandest gift is a large Gothic revival grandfather clock presented by 2,000 members of the first choir in the Philadelphia campaign in 1915. The Philadelphia revival had multiple choirs that rotated through the services, and at the conclusion of the campaign, members of the first choir pooled their resources to give the Sundays a gift that the couple could never forget. The chime heard every hour was to remind Billy and

EVERY MUSCLE IN HIS BODY PREACHES IN ACCORD WITH HIS VOICE.

FIGURE 20. *This cartoon dramatically illustrates Sunday's physical approach to preaching. From William Ellis's authorized biography published in 1914,* Billy Sunday: The Man and His Message.

FIGURE 21. *Clockwise from upper right: framed photograph of Cecil B. DeMille; oversized baseball gift; miniature coal mine lantern; presentation cocoa set;* Do Your Level Best; *Scranton, Pennsylvania, chauffeur loving cup. Items courtesy of the Billy Sunday Historic Site Museum, Winona Lake, Indiana.*

Nell of the city where they had spent the greatest amount of time for a revival campaign, a full eleven weeks.

The most common types of gifts to the Sundays were books and autographed photographs. Ninety-two books in the Sunday library were presented as gifts, most of which were given by the authors. *The Raven and the Chariot* by Elijah Brown was given in 1907 — seven years before his own biography of Billy Sunday was published. Ebenezer Lewis gave Sunday his self-published *Do Your Level Best,* the title of which became one of Sunday's favorite battle cries (fig. 21). The Woman's Christian Temperance Union (WCTU) of Allegheny County, Pennsylvania, presented Sunday with Ray Strachey's *Frances Willard: Her Life and Work,* and the Anti-Saloon League gave him its 1915 yearbook so that he might have access to the latest statistics in fighting the liquor lobby. Well over fifty autographed photographs were given to the Sundays from the likes of William "Buffalo Bill" Cody, John D. Rockefeller Sr., John Wanamaker, Charles E. Hughes, Bob Jones Sr., Charles Curtis, H. J. Heinz, the medical brothers C. H. and

W. A. Mayo, and Cecil B. DeMille, who inscribed over his photograph, "To the only man who works harder than I do" (fig. 21).

Traditional presentation pieces such as loving cups and silver serving utensils were numerous gifts. Loving cups from the students at Dartmouth College; a chauffeur delegation from Scranton, Pennsylvania (see figs. 1 and 21); Boy Scout troops; high school students; Kresge employees; and fraternal lodges represent just a few. Alongside these customary gifts were unique folk art pieces that reflected the lifestyles of the communities that produced them. A miniature coal miner's lantern from the DL&W Coal Mining Department that illuminates when filled with kerosene (fig. 21) and a photograph showing a carload of coal that arrived at the Winona Lake depot as a gift from the employees of the Pennsylvania Coal Company attest to Sunday's popularity in the mining district. A model boxcar from the Southern Railyard Shop employees held $346.75 of donations gathered by the South Carolinians for the preacher. A decoupage and wood-burn decorated plaque commemorating Sunday's revival in Sterling, Illinois, in 1904 is the oldest of such folk art pieces. Nearly 10 percent of the items in the home's collection fall into the category of gifts. This is a remarkably high percentage when considering that the bulk of the collection is composed of Sunday's personal library and other utilitarian items such as dinnerware and linens. Beyond shear volume, nearly all of the Sunday's most prestigious or expensive possessions are items received as gifts, a ringing endorsement of the public's esteem and affection.

Sitting on the Safety Valve

Trying to run a church without revivals can be
done — when you can run a gasoline engine on buttermilk.
—The Real Billy Sunday *(Brown)*

Gradually over time, Billy and Nell Sunday made a fundamental change in the organizational structure of the revival team. From 1896 to 1905, Billy organized the revivals principally by himself, with the assistance of a hired advance man and music leader. By 1906, Sunday's staff had grown to five or six, adding specialists in women's ministry, a secretary assistant, and a vocalist. Early on, Nell started offering help as an in absentia bookkeeper and trusted counselor to Billy, but by and large, she was not involved in the daily process of making the revival campaigns run smoothly. Her business savvy and administrative skills learned in her formative years were not being utilized to their fullest, and the couple decided that with their two older children off to private schools away from home, an opportunity arose for Nell to take on a more primary function in the revival organization. This was by no means a watershed moment, nor was it an easy decision. While it was true that the two eldest children were no longer underfoot by 1908, Billy Jr. had just turned six, and their youngest son, Paul, was still a one-year-old infant. As Nell's role in the revival campaigns increased, these two boys were left more and more often in the charge of grandparents or hired help. In 1911 Nell met Nora Lynn at the Erie, Pennsylvania, revival and struck a deal to secure her as their live-in housekeeper and nanny. With the addition of Nora Lynn, Nell was free to crisscross the country with her husband. This decision produced significant consequences both for the revivals and the Sunday family. Nell's positive impact in terms of increased numbers of conversions (appendix B) and free-will offerings was immediately evident. But on the family side of the coin, Billy and Nell later deeply regretted making this fundamental shift, not because of any shortcomings on the part of Nora Lynn but rather by witnessing the telltale signs of parental neglect when their children became adults. Ironically, Nell by this time was referred to more often as Ma Sunday, a nickname that Billy gave to her early in their marriage (fig. 22). Perhaps it was Billy's own sense of childhood neglect that led him to a mother figure for his mate. His sermons and possessions that related to the topic of womanhood also illuminate this sensitive subject. Ma made all personnel decisions, maintained the account books and cash flow, made initial and follow-up contacts for future revivals, reviewed tabernacle blueprints, approved site locations, and arranged for crowd control.[29] "Billy was my job," she said when interviewed in 1954, and on another occasion she remarked to the crowd gathered in the tabernacle, "My job is to sit on the safety valve."[30] In essence, she freed Billy to focus solely on his sermon development and presentation delivery.

One role of particular importance to Nell was in tabernacle planning and building. Sources conflict on the place and date of the first temporary tabernacle that Billy Sunday built as being either Elgin, Illinois, in 1900 or Perry, Iowa, in 1901. Accounts of the Perry tabernacle indicate that it was a crude structure that held about 1,000 people; even so, it served as the prototype for edifices that later became symbolic of a Sunday crusade. Sunday more often used tents for his meetings during this early phase of his career and utilized the temporary tabernacle form sparingly until October 1906, when a large tent collapsed after a freak overnight snowstorm during the last week of the Salida, Colorado, revival. Because Sunday's personal compensation offering was held the last few days of a revival, the collapsing of the tent created a crisis. Sunday had spent nearly three and a half weeks in Salida, yet without a venue for the final days, it was possible that he would leave with little or no financial return for his efforts. The local opera house was provided for his use at the eleventh hour, which cut his losses, but Billy and Nell had learned a valuable lesson. With the help of evangelist M. B. Williams, Billy and Nell came up with an ingenious plan for building a substantial, albeit temporary, venue in each city in which they held revivals.[31] The answer was the tabernacle.

The building of the tabernacle was in itself a clever promotional technique. In the days leading up to the revival, local citizens witnessed the erection of this gigantic structure on the outskirts of their town, foretelling Sunday's arrival on a grand scale. Even if a person did not particularly care to hear Sunday, the average citizen could hardly resist wanting to take a peek inside the largest arena he or she had ever seen or wondering who could possibly be important enough to warrant the building of such a structure. Tabernacles would range in size and could seat from 5,000 to 20,000 people. A Sunday staff member supervised the construction of the tabernacle, but volunteers, and in some instances even children, provided the labor (fig. 23). Billy Sunday tabernacles were built with tremendous speed in an era before strictly enforced building codes. Sunday was known to brag about the fact that "no board was held on with more than two nails." Never meant to be permanent, the enormous structures were usually torn down when the revival ended, and the lumber was sold to help defray any remaining expenses or to increase the revenues generated by the revival for the local churches.

Perhaps the most creative gift the Sundays ever received was a framed woodcut print of the interior of the Philadelphia tabernacle (fig. 24). This miniature drawing is an intricate piece of line art detailing the post and beam construction, the seating arrangements, and even the augaphone soundboard device suspended over the platform, which assisted

(opposite) FIGURE 22. *Billy and Nell Sunday at the peak of their popularity in 1917 had this image taken for circulation among the nation's press. This woman behind her man guided his every step. Image courtesy of the William and Helen Sunday Archives, Grace College, Winona Lake, Indiana.*

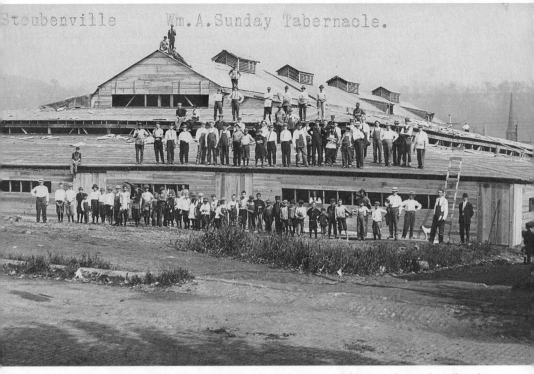

FIGURE 23. *Construction crew, including many children, at the Steubenville, Ohio, tabernacle in 1913. The raised roof vents and "frog-eye" dormers provided some ventilation, but Billy Sunday tabernacles were not built for comfort. Image courtesy of the William and Helen Sunday Archives, Grace College, Winona Lake, Indiana.*

in projecting Sunday's voice. The extraordinary frame, made from actual fragments of the Philadelphia tabernacle structure, is assembled in the shape of a window, thus providing the illusion of looking into the building to view the interior.

The change of format from tents to tabernacles necessitated longer revivals in larger cities, more elaborate organization, and, above all, dramatic increases in capital expenditures. The Sunday organization did not pay for the tabernacle. That expense, along with the salaries of paid staff members, had to be committed to and raised by the churches and the business leaders that banded together to bring Sunday to their city. In some instances, subscriptions of stock were even sold to help raise the initial funds necessary to book a six-to-eight-week revival (fig. 24). The sales pitch was that Sunday's influence would be so overwhelming

FIGURE 24. *Clockwise from upper right: Rainbow recording of "Calling Thee," Sunday stock certificate, folk art piece of Philadelphia tabernacle, photograph of Nell Sunday with Homer Rodeheaver, Elijah Brown's* The Real Billy Sunday, *Rodeheaver Company songbook* Victory Songs. *Items courtesy of the Billy Sunday Historic Site Museum, Winona Lake, Indiana.*

that church memberships would dramatically rise and employees would become more productive, thereby making the revival a sound spiritual and business investment. Most of the time this argument was not only persuasive, but to a large degree it was accurate. Only a handful of Sunday revivals ended in the red, and these were gladly underwritten by industrial leaders eager to see the benefits of Sunday's sermons upon their workforce.

During the years between 1910 and 1920, the money generated by the Sunday campaigns was enormous by any measure. Nell saw great marketing opportunities in the crowds that came to see her husband. Selling Bibles, songbooks, photographs, postcards, and sermon pamphlets at the tabernacle souvenir stand became a major source of the Sundays' income (fig. 25). Billy Sunday also earned royalties from his 1917 book, *Love Stories of the Bible,* and a 1914 biography by William Ellis, *Billy Sunday: The Man and His Message.* By far the hottest-selling item was Elijah Brown's biography, *The Real Billy Sunday* (fig. 24). Sales of this book were so great and so difficult to track accurately that Sunday bought the rights to the book from the author for $1,200 per year for the

FIGURE 25. *The souvenir stand at the back of a Sunday tabernacle circa 1915. Image courtesy of the William and Helen Sunday Archives, Grace College, Winona Lake, Indiana.*

remainder of Brown's life. Billy and Nell invested heavily in stocks and bonds, important certificates they kept in one of the two safes at Mount Hood. A wall safe is in the hall closet on the first floor, but the second and larger safe is a free-standing unit that bears "Reverend W. A. Sunday" in gold paint on the door over a decorative scene. Few ordinary citizens possessed their own safe. Fewer still had a need for more than one safe, and only America's elite had one with his or her name custom-painted on the door.

The Sundays' accumulation of wealth was easy fodder for critics, especially money known as a "love offering," the donation from each revival made specifically for the preacher's personal compensation. While it was true that the Sundays donated some of the largest love offerings, such as Chicago's and New York's, to charities, most of these donations went straight into the Sundays' bank accounts. From 1907 to 1918, he earned $1,139,315 from these offerings, nearly eighty-seven times the average worker's income of $13,000 during the same twelve years.[32] This level of income was unprecedented for a religious leader. It worried church officials, who feared preachers might demand higher salaries or, worse yet, take financial advantage of their position of influence. On more than one occasion, Sunday said at offering time, "Don't let me hear any coins fall into those buckets. I want to hear the rustle of paper."[33] Even though a statement such as this was never made with reference to his own compensation but rather to assist the local committee in gathering reimbursement of revival expenses, it was the zeal with which he pressured audiences to give money that bothered many.

Billy and Nell also developed a strong desire for the luxuries of life. The couple usually wore only the finest clothing, including expensive furs. A private Pullman railroad coach for the trip was often a prerequisite to obtaining a Sunday revival (fig. 26). At one point, the relationship was so strong that the Pullman Palace Car Company presented Billy and Nell with a plush armchair from one of its coaches in appreciation for the years of service commissioned by the traveling evangelist.

Criticisms and luxuries aside, Nell's impact on the scope of the revivals was almost immediate, and by 1912 she was the ever-present manager of what people were calling the Billy Sunday Machine. A major portion of Nell's time was spent in managing the cogs of this machine — the evangelistic team. Billy Sunday's evangelistic team varied in numbers from two to seventeen over the years, but this team commanded the attention of thousands of volunteers and paid temporary staff (appendix C). In the 1916 Boston campaign alone, 35,000 local people participated as ushers, choir members, security staff, and outreach workers. Keeping the team members happy and in line was easier said than done. The variety of tasks ranged from tabernacle construction supervisors to vocalists, from concessions operators to writers and outreach ministers.

Outside of Nell, one other constant remained during the peak twenty years of Billy Sunday's popularity, his music director, Homer Rodeheaver. Rodeheaver, known as Rody to his friends and admirers, was

Sunday's master of ceremonies as much as his choir director. Music was an incredibly important part of the Sunday show, and Rodeheaver, with his signature trombone in hand, would lead an assembly of voices 10,000 to 20,000 strong in old classics like "Onward Christian Soldier" or new standards such as "The Old Rugged Cross" or "Calling Thee," both of which Rodeheaver recorded with fellow Sunday team member vocalist Virginia Asher (fig. 24). The Sundays possessed forty-five of Rodeheaver's Rainbow Record label recordings, as well as an attractively framed and autographed photograph of Rodeheaver and a dozen of his books (hymnals, poetry books, and songbooks). He was also an accomplished storyteller, knowing precisely how to weave curiosity and irony, as witnessed in this yarn:

> Some years ago, Billy Sunday was conducting an evangelistic service in Duluth, Minnesota. A Jew was run over in the iron mines. They took him to a Catholic hospital, where an Episcopal doctor cut off his leg. A Presbyterian woman there, feeling sorry for the man, wrote to Dr. Barton, who was then running a Congregational paper in Chicago, and asked him to put an advertisement in his paper asking someone to donate a wooden leg to this Jew in the Catholic hospital, whose leg had been cut off by the Episcopal doctor.
>
> A Methodist woman in River Forest, Illinois, saw the advertisement in the Congregational paper. Her husband, who had been a Baptist and was dead, had a wooden leg. She telephoned for the Salvation Army Captain to come by and wrap up her Baptist husband's wooden leg. He took it down to the express office where a Lutheran express messenger delivered it to a Evangelical nurse in the Duluth office. She took it over to the Catholic hospital, and when they strapped it on this Jew, they said he had become a "United Brethren." This is the application of cooperation.[34]

In the late 1920s Sunday's old friend started to see certain elements of the revival going astray. Chief among Rodeheaver's concerns were Sunday's increased length of sermons, the speed with which he delivered

(opposite) FIGURE 26. *Private Pullman rail car transporting the Sunday party circa 1909. B. D. Ackley at front left, Fred Fischer with book, Charles Butler wearing white vest, Sunday seated at desk, Clifton Pryor Pledger seated behind Sunday, daughter Helen Edith, and son George at front right. Image courtesy of the William and Helen Sunday Archives, Grace College, Winona Lake, Indiana.*

them (so much so that Sunday's audience often could not understand what he was saying), and his lack of clarity when asking for the altar call. Rodeheaver was also alarmed by Sunday's assertive manner in requesting monetary offerings. Sunday's incessant pacing on the platform while Rodeheaver led the choir frustrated the music director and made him feel less than appreciated for his vital role in priming the crowd for Sunday's message. Rodeheaver crafted a letter constructively outlining these concerns in July 1927; however, it never reached Sunday. Nell intercepted the letter and informed Rodeheaver that she had no intention of giving it to Billy because it would only make matters worse and the situation more tense.[35] Within a year, Homer Rodeheaver quietly left the Sunday organization. After a couple of years of bitter feelings, the three old friends made amends, and one of the most recent photographs in the collection is of Nell Sunday and Homer Rodeheaver walking the grounds of Winona Lake shortly before his death in 1955 (fig. 24).

Chapter 4
For the Love of a Nation

To understand the unique perspective that a material culture approach offers this investigation, it is worthwhile to briefly contrast the methods of such an approach with those of a conventional historical analysis. The historical interpretation of people, places, and events has traditionally been based upon research in written documents or oral traditions. Recorded accounts can capture infinite levels of minute detail. While the written word is unquestionably powerful in this regard, it also has its limitations. First, mistakes in written records do occur, and the historians of today read and rely on these mistaken accounts of the past. Thus it is now considered a standard practice to obtain a consensus of accounts from different sources before a historian places a stamp of approval on any explanation of a past event.

Second, not all human behavior is recorded with the same level of coverage or precision. With the proliferation of written documentation, especially in the last two centuries, some of these gaps in recording human behavior are starting to diminish. These vast increases in the production of written records, however, still do not always result in an equitable distribution of perspectives. As has always been the problem, the recorded opinions of the few sometimes appear more important and widespread than they usually are in reality. Authors' biases are inextricably linked to their prose, and this work is certainly no exception. These biases, however, are often ignored by the readers, and written documentation assumes a sense of truth sometimes too powerful to overcome. In delving into the topics of this chapter, politics and reform, written accounts are numerous, and it is precisely on this ocean of rhetoric that material culture evidence may shed brilliant new light.

Some of the biggest lies ever told are to be found on gravestones.

—THE REAL BILLY SUNDAY *(Brown)*

Mixing Religion and Politics

A painted fire never boiled an egg.—Billy Sunday Speaks!

For Billy Sunday, the line between religious morals and political action was blurry, if it existed at all. Politics was simply morals put into action, and if there was any place on the American landscape that needed a healthy dose of revivalism, it was, in Sunday's opinion, the legislative chambers of statehouses and Capitol Hill. Although Sunday never ran for elected office, he maintained close contact with those who did, for he knew that if his reforms were to be enacted, they must pass through elected officials first. If that required crossing party lines or stepping on political toes, Billy Sunday did whatever was necessary to get his reforms passed. He took his issues of women's suffrage, sex education in public schools, and the banning of amusements to the ears of city mayors, governors, state legislators, members of Congress, and even presidents.

It is not surprising that presidents wanted to befriend Sunday given the influence that he wielded among the common citizens. Sunday had autographed photographs from William H. Taft, Warren G. Harding, Calvin Coolidge, and Herbert Hoover. Correspondence came from many of the same individuals, as well as Theodore Roosevelt, and a five-volume set of *History of the American People*, personally signed in 1916 by its author, Woodrow Wilson, was a gift from the New Jersey state government (fig. 27). In the years following Sunday's death, Harry S. Truman and Dwight D. Eisenhower sent photographs and gifts to Nell Sunday, although she decided to hide Truman's photo behind a picture of the 1950s baseball commissioner Ford Frick because of ongoing tensions between the Sunday household and Franklin Delano Roosevelt's former vice president (fig. 27). In fact, every U.S. president from 1900 through 1960 is represented by a personal gift or memento in the home. That said, the only artifact in the Sunday collection from FDR was the telegram of condolence to Nell following Billy's death in 1935. FDR was the incarnation of many causes Sunday fought against. First, Roosevelt made good on his campaign promise to sign the repeal of the Prohibition amendment immediately after taking office. Second, and almost as bad in Sunday's eyes, Roosevelt's New Deal programs appeared to be dangerously socialistic, with a large, centralized federal government taking charge of fixing people's problems instead of citizens seeking solutions on their own in a free-market economy or, better yet, through

FIGURE 27. *Clockwise from upper left: framed photo of Harry S. Truman, bronze bust of Abraham Lincoln, framed souvenir drawing New York City campaign,* Christ and the World at War, The Devil and the Kaiser, The United States in Prophecy, *U.S. Army soldier's New Testament, Liberty Loan speaker ribbon,* Back to the Republic, The Red Network, History of the American People. *Items courtesy of the Billy Sunday Historic Site Museum, Winona Lake, Indiana.*

salvation in Christ. When Sunday saw a picture of FDR in the newspaper, he saw red.

Socialism and communism, two political ideals that Sunday never found a real need to distinguish between, were in his opinion merely a human effort to run the world better than God. What made these movements most troubling to Sunday was that as one moved farther to the political left, God became a smaller player in the lives of citizens. For Sunday, it was blasphemous to attempt to replace God with well-informed will. Godlessness meant eternal damnation, and that was reason enough to despise left-wing ideals. As in the case with evolution, he studied the problem from the inside out. Sunday used *What Is Socialism?* by James E. Le Rossignol extensively and kept a copy of *Russia under the Hammer and Sickle* by Ralston Purina executive William H. Danforth, as well as Albion W. Small's *Between Eras from Capitalism to Democracy,* to delve into the subtleties of liberal paradigms. The age of social reform in the first two decades of the twentieth century was not without its critics.

FIGURE 28. *Billy Sunday giving a stump speech for President Herbert Hoover's reelection campaign in 1932. Image courtesy of the William and Helen Sunday Archives, Grace College, Winona Lake, Indiana.*

While Sunday was indeed a reformer himself, his reforms were meant to take the country back to a more conservative Puritan lifestyle of strait-laced behavior. Albert C. Rightor's *Fallacies of Our National Government* and Harry F. Atwood's *Back to the Republic* point toward Sunday's apprehension of the new, more powerful government (fig. 27). If society was to become better, it would result from the accumulation of more saved souls.[1]

It certainly got under Sunday's skin more than once that Indiana, the same state he called home, also spawned one of the greatest socialist leaders of the country, Eugene V. Debs. To say that the two men did not like each other is a gigantic understatement. "We look upon Billy Sunday as a vulgar harlequin, a ranting mountebank who, in the pay of plutocracy, prostitutes religion to perpetuate hell on earth," Debs said on one occasion.[2] For Sunday's part, he proclaimed, "I have no use for these intellectual engineers who try to chart man's pathway through the sin-cursed world by the compass of their opinions."[3] Socialists, to him, were "God-forsaken anarchists, those agitators that spew out and stir up trouble."[4] *The Red Network* by Elizabeth Dilling gave him the tools to ferret out these dissenters and expose their methods of operation (fig. 27).

Championing social reform necessarily meant political involvement for Billy Sunday. His last great political stand was undoubtedly his worst thought out, if he hoped to maintain any semblance of popularity. Sunday decided to campaign hard for his friend Herbert Hoover in both the 1928 election, which Hoover won, and his bid for reelection in 1932 (fig. 28). It was the 1932 campaign that especially damaged Sunday's popularity. Sunday could not win votes even from his most ardent supporters, who had stuck with him from the glory years of the 1910s through the tribulations of 1920s secularism. Armed with a 1930 copy of *The Hoover Administration: Its Policies and Its Achievements in the First Sixteen Months*, published by the Republican National Committee, as well as numerous letters from either Hoover himself or his personal secretary, Everett Sanders, Sunday was ready to fight for the honor of his friend and the Republican Party. In the end, the economy spoke louder than any of the candidates, and Billy Sunday, already viewed by some as a relic, now was perceived by most as a relic who backed a loser.

Sunday philosophically identified with the Republican Party at an early age in his life. His father had died for the Union flag, and there always existed an implied perception that the Republican Party was more strongly Christian than the Democratic Party. As a staunch Republican, Sunday's greatest political hero was naturally Abraham Lincoln. A large lithograph print of Lincoln and a companion piece of Ulysses S. Grant adorned the walls of the master bedroom. John G. Nicolay's *A Short Life of Abraham Lincoln* reviewed the slain president's legacy. A bronze and marble bust of Lincoln maintained a prominent place in the inglenook, the heart of the home (fig. 27). Symbolically, for many Americans Lincoln was the Christ figure for the nation. While a parallel relationship in American history also exists with George Washington, who, like Moses, led his people from bondage, Lincoln, like Christ, was the savior (of the Union), giving his life at the moment of triumph. The fact that Lincoln died on Good Friday is, for some religious historians, too great a coincidence to ignore. He freed the slaves, albeit with motives scholars still debate, but Billy Sunday's view of Lincoln was clean, pure, and unadulterated. Lincoln had saved the young nation from itself, and Sunday, too, would rise up to rescue his nation when crisis threatened.

Uncle Sam's Pinch Hitter

Christianity and Patriotism are synonymous terms, and hell and traitors are synonymous. —Billy Sunday Was His Real Name (*McLoughlin*)

In the spring of 1917 the United States entered into a crisis of Billy Sunday–style proportions, the Great War. It so happened that Sunday was just about to launch one of the greatest campaigns of his life in New York City when news broke of America's involvement. Expenses for the ten-week New York City crusade were paid in their entirety by the Sundays' good friend John D. Rockefeller Jr.[5] Sunday's New York City tabernacle, second in size only to Chicago's, which was three feet longer, was nicknamed the Glory Barn.[6] It measured 84,968 square feet, could seat nearly 20,000 people, and required 400,000 feet of lumber and 250 barrels of nails during construction. Conservative estimates projected that he spoke to nearly a quarter of the city's population of five million, and the "city of sin" gave him his single largest love offering of his career. Sunday made the grand gesture of donating his entire earnings from that campaign, $120,500, to the YMCA and the Red Cross to assist with the war effort.[7] During the war years, he set up army and navy recruiting stations next to his tabernacles.[8] Sunday spoke at rallies to enlist volunteers and inspired troops before they shipped off (fig. 29). He tried his best to obtain an officer's commission for his oldest son, George, as evidenced by numerous letters to high-ranking officials in Congress and the War Department. A certificate of membership in the American Defense Society and a Liberty Loan Speaker ribbon showed that Sunday was hardly shy about raising financial support (fig. 27), but by all accounts his greatest impact during the war was the adamant vocal support that he gave day in and day out at his campaigns. He denounced Kaiser Wilhelm and the German people in general as being vile, subhuman demons. For these vitriolic railings, he drew from *Christ and the World at War* by Basil Matthews, *The Devil and the Kaiser* by Lincoln McConnell, *Voices of Our Leaders* by William Mather Lewis, and a little book of poetry entitled *Alas! I Am a Prussian* by J. A. J. Tibbals (fig. 27).

Sunday's words cut deep wounds in the German American community, and many saw his marauding of Germany as an opportunistic slam against the country that had tormented him for so many years. Germans

FIGURE 29. *Billy Sunday sends the troops off with a rally in 1918 at the Naval Training Station in Newport, Rhode Island. Image courtesy of the William and Helen Sunday Archives, Grace College, Winona Lake, Indiana.*

were brewers by tradition, and the European country had spawned some of the greatest minds in the late nineteenth and early twentieth centuries in the fields of mathematics, science, medicine, philosophy, and psychology. Several of these thinkers, such as Karl Marx, Friedrich Nietzsche, and Sigmund Freud, had planted what Sunday considered to be the devil's seeds in the human mind. A chance for America to fight Germany was almost too good for Sunday to believe. With Germany publicly perceived as the aggressor, Sunday could let loose with all of his years of pent-up fury. He justified Americans' right to kill Germans as "good versus evil," even though he kept a copy of *An Appeal against Slaughter* by Marion E. Coville in his bookcase. This book, however, unlike most books in his library, did not appear to receive much use. Ironically, Sunday's own family heritage traced back to German immigrants. His great-grandfather, born Heinrich Sundag, was going by the name Henry Sunday in 1822, and every succeeding generation kept the Americanized version.

Billy Sunday wrapped himself in the American flag when he gave patriotic speeches and waved a gigantic star-spangled banner from side to side over the crowd in his tabernacles while Homer Rodeheaver led the group in "The Battle Hymn of the Republic" or "America."[9] Sunday had at his disposal Henry Fowler's *Patriotic Orations* to provide assistance if he needed any, but more than likely he came up with his own original material for these speeches, which he so enthusiastically delivered. Several items from this period, either given as gifts or purchased by the Sundays, bear the American flag. A hand-drawn plaque of Sunday in front of Old Glory and a poem about the flag, "Here's to the Red of It," are two examples of patriotic artifacts from the war era (fig. 27). Dozens of flags and bunting banners draped from the crests of his tabernacles inside and out.

More than just a cause for flag-waving, the threat from Germany, for Sunday, was very real and perhaps an apocalyptic sign. In 1918 the Philadelphia Prophetic Conference considered the serious possibility that the war in Europe was the realization of the book of Revelation — the beginning of the end of the world. The conference published its proceedings, *Light on Prophecy*, and Sunday not only kept a copy, but he made numerous notes and reader's marks in it, suggesting that he was actively using the text as a source for sermon material. *The United States in Prophecy* by J. C. Kellogg addressed this possibility as well (fig. 27). Even after the war was over, Sunday's fascination with it continued. He had autographed photographs from General John "Black Jack" Pershing and other notable war heroes. He obtained an olive-drab soldier's New Testament as a remembrance of the modern crusade, as well as books on the history of the war, such as *Belgium* by Brand Whitlock and *Red and Me*, a soldier's memoir by Joseph A. Hardesty.

The First World War, like the quest to prohibit alcohol, fit snugly within Billy Sunday's agenda for making America a better place. When Sunday announced in 1918 that he planned to go to France to support the troops, Woodrow Wilson personally asked him to stay stateside, support America's cause through political speeches, and promote the sale of Liberty Bonds.[10] While Sunday always politically preferred Republicans to Democrats, he honored Wilson's request as only Billy Sunday could. Instead of showing embarrassment from the president's instructions, Sunday turned the matter into a sacrificial act of patriotism, letting everyone know that staying on the home front was not his first choice, but he would serve his commander in chief and obey his orders. The war had been a great opportunity for Sunday to perform on the national political stage, and he excelled. Following the war, a reactionary wave of secularism began to distance Sunday from his once-adoring public and eroded his political clout. It seemed that as the nation's fears subsided, so waned the impassioned support of Billy Sunday. Indirectly, Nell noted this inverse relationship in a 1954 interview: "I thank God for allowing me the privilege of living to see the day when evangelism is coming up. It went down for twenty years — down, down, down — between those two wars."[11]

Society's Ills

The best time for a man to sow his wild oats is between the ages
of eighty-five and ninety. —Twenty Years with Billy Sunday (*Rodeheaver*)

Billy Sunday's library contains no less than 600 publications dealing with historical and contemporary Christianity. Considering his melding of social reform, politics, and religion, the Christian authors who bore significant influence upon Sunday merit closer examination. The majority of his books about religion exhibit all the hallmarks of having been read, such as turned-down page corners and inserted bookmarks. Many bear the marks of Sunday's own pencil, including frantically underlined text and his recognizable all-capital letter script in the margins. By knowing what Sunday read and how he used what he read in his sermons, we can learn a great deal about what made him tick. His material possessions bear witness to the fact that he was well equipped to develop opinions on the hottest issues of the day, including the shift in cultural values of Western civilization, labor unrest, evolution, the changing role of women in American society, and contemporary Christian interpretation. The issues were complex. Only his answers were simple.

From a material perspective, there was no greater influence theologically on Billy Sunday than the nineteenth-century preacher Dwight L. Moody. Sunday possessed seven texts that either were written by Moody or were biographical accounts of Moody's life. Books by Moody, including *Moody's Great Sermons,* posthumously published in 1900 (fig. 30); *Pleasure and Profit in Bible Study*; *To the Work*; and *Prevailing Prayer: What Hinders It?* provide direct links to Sunday's strict adherence to biblical text. Sunday was, of course, under the influence of Moody from the moment he was converted. The Pacific Garden Mission and the Chicago YMCA were both guided, in large part, by Moody's teachings at his institute in Chicago. Sunday's mentor, J. Wilbur Chapman, had a close relationship with Moody and in 1877 met with the great evangelist to gain insights for his own career through Moody's counsel.[12] *The Life of D. L. Moody* by his son, William R. Moody, and *Moody's Anecdotes & Illustrations* by J. B. McClure provided Sunday with biographical outlines of his hero.

FIGURE 30. *Clockwise from the top: Poland Springs water bottle, phonograph record "The Naughty Waltz,"* The Working Man and Social Problems, *WCTU life membership certificate, cigar band folk art ring dish,* Instead of Wild Oats, *cordial glasses,* Moody's Great Sermons, *brandy snifter. Items courtesy of the Billy Sunday Historic Site Museum, Winona Lake, Indiana.*

Sunday's sermons reflected his admiration for Moody in that he was the most cited and lauded preacher Sunday ever discussed. A third biography, George T. B. Davis's *Dwight L. Moody: The Man and His Mission,* bears a striking resemblance on the surface to *Billy Sunday: The Man and His Message,* a 1914 authorized biography by William T. Ellis. It hardly seems accidental that the two biography titles are so similar; Sunday idolized Moody, and many compared the two directly. Both were premillennialists, stressing the importance of accepting the salvation of Christ now due to the imminence of his second coming. Departing from the stricter versions of premillennialist thought in which the cleansing of the world for Christ's return bore little importance, as seen in A. B. Simpson's *The Coming One* and C. F. Wimberly's *Behold the Morning,* both Moody and Sunday strongly advocated social reforms that led people away from the path of sin. Chief among these reforms were temperance, self-control over sins of the flesh, and societal abolition of amusement temptations. These social reforms were bolstered with books in the Sunday library, such as *After Prison . . . What?* by Maud Ballington Booth, *Christianity and the Social Crisis* by Walter Rauschenbusch, *Writings of a Roadman* by G. W. Hootman, and James F. Oates's *The Religious Condition of Young Men.*

American society, Sunday believed, was in deep trouble. Soft ministers preaching a nonliteral, watered-down brand of Christian ideals were leading the country down a dead-end alley toward hell. J. C. Brown's *The Oxford Group Movement: Is It of God or Satan?* provided the answer Sunday longed to trumpet — the Social Gospel was a wolf in sheep's clothing. Sunday drew extensively from *Lectures to Young Men* by Henry Ward Beecher, *The Working Man and Social Problems* by Charles Stelzle (fig. 30), and Elmer Ellsworth Higley's *The Sterile Soul.* For Sunday, original sin, which came at birth, was easier to deal with than the sin committed by a conscious human mind. The church could forgive the infant of original sin, but getting men and women to refrain from sinning anew was something else.

Other evangelists whose works Sunday possessed and used extensively included C. H. Spurgeon, R. A. Torrey, and Charles G. Finney, the founder of Oberlin College. Finney's works, *Lectures on Revival of Religion* and *Sermons on Gospel Themes*, focused on the power of Scripture and the preacher's role in harnessing that power. *How to Bring Men to Christ, Real Salvation, The Bible and Its Christ,* and *The Gospel for Today,* all authored by Sunday's contemporary R. A. Torrey, delved deeply into the psychological benefits of Christian beliefs in American society at the turn of the twentieth century. Spurgeon gave Sunday a wealth of sermon material upon which he drew in crafting his own talks, including *Spurgeon's Gold, John Ploughman's Talk,* and *Morning & Evening Daily Readings.* Sunday looked to J. H. Jowett's *Preacher: His Life and Work* to guide his own standards and principles, and he always kept his well-worn copy of *Gipsy Smith: An Autobiography* close by.

Several texts in Sunday's library sound the alarm of changing times, such as *Can Organized Religion Survive?* by Oswald J. Smith and J. C. Kellogg's *The Tec-noc-crazy Old World.* Such books reinforced his belief that the world was quickly becoming a colder, more complicated place. He used these books and others to build his sermons in the same way a lawyer builds a case. Several of these societal changes were related to the subject of amusements, such as theater, cards, music, and dance. Sunday drew from Harry Brolaski's *The Fool and His Money; The Worldly Christian's Trinity,* anonymously authored by "A Harassed Pastor"; and

Popular Amusements: Destructive and Constructive, collectively written by Lee Ralph Phipps, John Emory Roberts, and DeWitt Miley Phipps. These vices were on the lips of nearly every preacher, and while Sunday was not alone in denouncing them, he was likely the most forceful voice in the nation advocating abolishment of these practices.

The dance hall and the ballroom were two of Billy's favorite targets. However, several artifacts in the Sunday home strongly contradict his public stance on dance. The Sundays had a large, top-of-the-line Victrola phonograph and a sizable collection of records. Thirty-six of the phonograph records are classified as dance music, such as "The Naughty Waltz" by Olive Kline and Elsie Baker (fig. 30), "I Might Be Your Once-in-a-While" by the Yerkes Jazarimba Orchestra, and "Love Bird" by the Casino Dance Orchestra. Still more shocking are the selections classed as blues or jazz, such as "Loose Feet" by the Tampa Blue Jazz Band, "Great White Way Blues" by Ladd's Black Aces, and "Baby Blue Eyes" by Baily's Lucky Seven — quite a medley of melodies for a preacher who called dance "the dry-rot of society."[13] A full 20 percent of the record collection falls into the category of dance or risqué music. The possibility remains that these records belonged to Billy and Nell's children, but if such were the case, why would Billy and Nell keep such "vile" material around their home after the children moved out? From a material standpoint, one cannot rule out the strong possibility that Billy and Nell played and enjoyed these songs.

Sunday championed several controversial causes, such as women's suffrage and sex education, and in doing so he went much farther in terms of social reform than Moody. While *Memories of Mother* by Rennetts C. Miller and Nixon Waterman's *The Girl Wanted* depict a Victorian romanticized view of women's role in contemporary society, T. DeWitt Talmage's pioneering work, *Woman: Her Power and Privileges*, presented a more assertive picture of womanhood. Sunday employed women extensively in his campaigns, providing special Bible study classes for women in all walks of life. Women working as stenographers, clerks, and bookkeepers met with Sunday staffers at noon-hour luncheons. Other female assistants on Sunday's team took the message directly to the women working in factories. Housemaids and schoolgirls met after hours with assistants, and women of high social standing were asked to hold luncheons and teas as a forum for Billy or Nell to speak.[14] Sunday even had special "women only" sermons, in which he drew upon the vast literature of sexual virtue and the value of discretion (fig. 31). To make his point, Sunday pulled material

BACK FROM THE WOMEN'S MEETING

FIGURE 31. *Cartoon from 1910 of the reaction after a "women only" meeting at the Sunday tabernacle. Image courtesy of the William and Helen Sunday Archives, Grace College, Winona Lake, Indiana.*

from *Sexual Knowledge* and *Reproduction and Sexual Hygiene*, both by Winfield S. Hall. He also relied on Jeannette Winter Hall's *Life's Story: A Book for Girls* and Mary Wood-Allen's *Almost a Woman*. In the face of knowing the dangers of sin, Sunday wondered how any sane woman could not choose to become an upstanding wife and mother. Kathleen Norris's *Mother: A Story* and Mary L. Read's *The Mothercraft Manual* drove home the conservative point that women could best serve humankind by being good mothers.

In the same manner, Sunday addressed the "men only" meetings with straightforward talk about the consequences of the sins inherent to human flesh. Homer Rodeheaver recalled how time and again he witnessed two to eight men faint during the same portion of Sunday's sermon called "The Devil's Boomerang."[15] For the men's meeting, Sunday pulled information from *The Voyage of Life: Manhood* by W. W. Everts, *Instead of Wild Oats* by Winfield S. Hall (fig. 30), *Problems of Manhood* by James M. Taylor, and *The Secrets of Success for Boys and Young Men* by B. J. Kendall. Realizing the positive impact made by these sex education meetings in his campaigns, Sunday controversially sought to employ their lessons in public schools. His goal remained simple in concept. If the truth about human nature was exposed completely and secrecy dispelled, only a fool would choose sin over clean living.

Demon Rum

I'm going to fight the liquor business till hell freezes over,
and then I'll put on ice skates and fight it some more.
—Billy Sunday (*Lockerbie*)

According to numerous written accounts in the form of newspaper columns, popular magazine articles, and biographies, Billy Sunday's greatest cure to the ills of humankind was the saving power of Jesus Christ. One dark enemy stood in the way of Sunday's succeeding with his main cause, demon alcohol. Records document his long personal experience with liquor, especially during his baseball days. Drinking and getting drunk were as much a part of the ballplayer's lifestyle as traveling from city to city. Sunday recounted in one of his sermons how hard drinking cut short the lives of many of his former teammates on the Chicago White Stockings.[16] For nearly every evil act in the world, Sunday could find a connection to alcohol. Alcohol made men commit crimes, made women lose their virtue, and robbed children of their innocence. His most famous sermon, "Get on the Water Wagon," became a favorite American catch-phrase — one was either "on the wagon" (dry) or "off the wagon" (wet). The water wagon gave the ex-drinker a symbolic free ride to sobriety. This sermon, colloquially known as the "Booze Sermon," was more than a mere fist-pounding denunciation of whiskey as the devil's blood. Sunday blitzed his audience with facts and figures similar to those used in sociological studies of his day. He cited the economic drain that alcohol consumption placed on the nation, the physical damage it wreaked on the human body, and the debilitating effects it had on moral behavior. He quoted everything from the U.S. Department of Agriculture to the *Saturday Evening Post*, building a mountain of economic and moral evidence against the vile effects of alcohol on humankind. Sunday used the sermon at every revival until Prohibition was enacted, and even after the Eighteenth Amendment took effect, he reworked the sermon to ensure that Prohibition would remain the law of the land. He was a powerful speaker, as witnessed in his opening paragraph of "Get on the Water Wagon":

> I am the sworn, eternal, uncompromising enemy of the Liquor Traffic. I ask no quarter and I give none. I have drawn the sword in defense of God, home, wife, children, and native land, and I will never sheathe it until the undertaker pumps me full of embalming fluid, and if my wife is alive, I think I shall call her to my bedside and say: "Nell, when I am dead, send for the butcher and skin me, and have my hide tanned and made into drum heads, and hire men to go up and down the land and beat the drums and say, 'My husband, Bill Sunday, still lives and gives the whiskey gang a run for its money.'"[17]

For Sunday, alcohol was a material tool of the devil and, when combined with gambling and other vices, ready at any instant to send the morally weak down a path of sin (fig. 32). Billy Sunday promised that all of the nation's modern problems of poverty, increased crime, unstable markets, domestic violence, moral decay, labor unrest, and foreign immigration would be cured if the country would simply remove the presence of alcohol. During his Memphis campaign in the mid-1920s, Sunday even went on a still raid with a local sheriff in the hills north of the city. The event, recorded by a local reporter and later published in *Scribner's Magazine*, demonstrated the delight that Sunday expressed in locating and destroying a whiskey still and apprehending the moonshiners.[18] For Sunday, a man who seldom went camping or fishing, going after a moonshiner was the ultimate big-game hunt (fig. 33).

FIGURE 32. *A front-page cartoon from the* Atlanta Constitution *in 1917 of Sunday's war against the devil and sinful vices. Image courtesy of the William and Helen Sunday Archives, Grace College, Winona Lake, Indiana.*

FIGURE 33. *Cartoon of Sunday battling illegal blind tiger operations during the Prohibition era in 1928. Sunday, playing the role of third base coach, is fooling the tiger by waving him on, knowing full well that the relay throw from "St. Louis" will put the tiger out at home. Image courtesy of the William and Helen Sunday Archives, Grace College, Winona Lake, Indiana.*

Temperance was the one political cause for which Billy Sunday was a true national leader. Not surprisingly, he often coordinated his campaigns for achieving this lofty goal in cities and states where local or state Prohibition options were on the ballot. "I'm going to make this place so dry, they'll have to prime a man to spit," was a familiar epigram from Sunday when he arrived in a new town.[19] Many credit Sunday with singlehandedly generating the energy to win statewide dry options in both Michigan and Colorado.[20] The state of Colorado even dedicated a song to Sunday in 1914 entitled "John Barleycorn Goodbye!" by Les Wallace, Josiah Maloney, and Robert Sharp (fig. 34). In 1915 he teamed up with quadrennial Democratic presidential candidate William Jennings Bryan to lead a nationwide campaign for temperance.[21] Sunday reached more people individually with his Booze Sermon than Bryan, Frances Willard, Carry Nation, and William E. "Pussyfoot" Johnson talked to in their combined lifetimes. By 1915 Sunday had spoken to nearly forty million people, and more came to see him every day. For weeks at a time, as many as 50,000 people a day heard him preach on the evil of liquor.[22] No one else commanded numbers like that — not entertainers, not even presidents. At times, he did have defeats, most notably the Chicago revival of 1918.[23] At a time when the Prohibition movement was at its fever pitch and Sunday was for all practical purposes "coming home" to America's second city, his Chicago campaign proved a disappointment when compared to those in New York, Boston, or Philadelphia. Years later, Frank Sinatra was right. Chicago was the town that Billy Sunday could not shut down.

Sunday maintained a number of texts in his library to support his position on temperance. The *American Prohibition Year Book for 1904,* compiled by Alonzo E. Wilson; George M. Hammel's *The Passing of the Saloon*; and Samuel R. Altman's *The Legalized Outlaw* were part of Sunday's early self-education on the subject. R. J. Patterson's *Catch-My-Pal*; *The Anti-Saloon League Year Book for 1915,* compiled by Earnest Hurst Cherrington; and *How to Live,* coauthored by Irving Fisher and Eugene Lyman Fisk, gave Sunday more ammunition to hurl at saloon keepers and brewers during the tremendous political push for temperance in the 1910s. A 1916 certificate attests to his life membership in the WCTU (fig. 30). For Sunday, however, the liquor problem was not only a boil on America's neck but also a moral war fought for men and women the world over. This broad perspective is a central theme in two books Sunday referenced often, Randolph Wellford Smith's *The Sober*

FIGURE 34. *Sheet music "John Barleycorn — Goodbye!" credits Billy Sunday with making Colorado dry. Image courtesy of the William and Helen Sunday Archives, Grace College, Winona Lake, Indiana.*

World and Earnest Hurst Cherrington's *America and the World Liquor Problem.*

But did Billy Sunday live the life he preached? Several artifacts present conflicting evidence. There are no hidden bottles of wine or whiskey anywhere in the dark corners of the attic or basement. But there are bottles of a different kind — cases of Poland Springs bottled water from Maine (fig. 30). Oral tradition maintains that Sunday had a sensitive stomach and drank two quarts of Poland Springs water every day to sustain good health.[24] Bottled water became widely marketed during the Prohibition era as an alternative to previously bottled alcoholic beverages. In fact, the Poland Springs water at Mount Hood was bottled by the distillers Hiram Walker and Sons, who adapted to nonalcoholic beverages in order to stay in business during the 1920s. These cases of bottled water symbolically reflect Sunday's success in achieving a nationwide "water wagon," and he played off this connection by doing his part to make bottled water appear stylish. In similar fashion, a set of three Welch's Grape Juice shot glasses from the 1920s demonstrate the industry's ability to adapt to the new national edict and capitalize on new market frontiers. These glasses are far too small to be considered traditional juice glasses, and in their size and shape they obviously resemble their spirit-carrying ancestors. Welch's marketing goal with these glasses was to give its consumers the psychological buzz of imbibing forbidden fruit while maintaining 200-proof legality. In 1915 grape juice became the battle cry for the temperance movement when, during the course of a typical William Jennings Bryan "dry" speech, a chorus of voices yelled:

> William, William Jennings Bryan
> William, William Jennings Bryan
> William, William Jennings Bryan
> We'll all drink grape juice yet![25]

Sunday's ownership of these items may be justified on the grounds that he was supporting the country's efforts to adapt to the new law. If the old distillers still turned a profit by bottling nonalcoholic drinks or the public wanted to pretend that they were drinking something other than grape juice, Billy Sunday probably did not care — for if no one was producing or drinking alcohol, the nation's collective behavior, in his opinion, was better for it.

Eight other artifacts in Sunday's possession create a greater conflict with his public stance on alcohol consumption. A single wine glass, three brandy snifters, and a set of two cordial glasses are all unmistakable receptacles for alcoholic beverages (fig. 30). The intended use for these items, all found far back in the depths of the china cupboard (and thus well away from public view), appears obvious. What is not so clear is whether the Sundays actually used these glasses for their common purpose. Though one will probably never know for certain, a number of nagging questions are raised by the presence of these artifacts. Why would Sunday even possess brandy snifters? Whether they were used for brandy or soft drinks, the symbolic message inherent in the shape of a brandy snifter is as distinct as a beer mug. A folk art ring dish decorated with cigar bands and cigar box die-cut decorations, possibly used as an ashtray, raises a few more eyebrows (fig. 30). Sunday's position on tobacco use was nearly as strong as his denunciation of alcohol. Yet a popular dance record in the Sundays' Victrola, "Down By the Winegar Woiks" by Aileen Stanley and Billy Murray, references social use of both alcohol and tobacco.

Just as the fictional young preacher Elmer Gantry was warned by Bishop Aberman to avoid at all costs "the very appearance of evil," Sunday, too, must have been aware that public perception is just as important as actual circumstances, and in some cases is more important.[26] Why risk having a pair of cordial glasses, albeit ones with nicely etched berries and leaves, if it meant the potential downfall of one's reputation? Stories of Sunday drinking at high-profile summer parties and of wine bottles being strewn behind the Sunday home on weekends, viewed by many as the tall tales of a few cranks with an ax to grind, may have some credence in the light of such damning material evidence. While these artifacts do not represent the majority of objects in the collection that are consistent with his public position, these items nonetheless call into question the possibility of any conclusive answer on the subject of Sunday's personal use of alcohol.

Chapter 5
At Home in Winona Lake

The central tenet of the material culture approach is that past human behavior is directly embedded into physical objects that survive over time. An artifact carries with it the thoughts and ideas of its maker through its shape, texture, color, and composition. These characteristics are material representations of the maker's mental constructs and, as such, provide a semipermanent remnant of a past thought or action. In a world of mass-produced goods, the presence or absence of possessions purchased by an individual provides insights into the purchaser's desires, attitudes, values, and preferences in a world full of choices. Items received as gifts that remain in an individual's possession primarily represent the values and attitudes of the giver(s). However, the fact that a gift stays in the recipient's possession implies at least tacit acceptance and approval of the values and attitudes embedded in the object.

Another advantage in studying material culture is that artifacts generally possess no second-party interpretive biases, such as those found in written accounts. Because the material item exemplifies intact manifestations of a past event, an artifact is considered the most primary of sources and, in some ways, more reliable than first-person accounts. Material culture presents the viewer with "solid evidence" of past lifestyles and events and empowers the viewer to make his or her own interpretations based upon personal observation. In the case of the Sunday family collection, museum visitors today are given this unique opportunity, for the vast majority of the Sundays' material culture remains exposed and available for firsthand observation on a daily basis.

America's Christian Playground

You cannot keep a rose in the ground if the root is healthy.
When God kisses the spot with sunshine and rain it bursts forth.
—Twenty Years with Billy Sunday (*Rodeheaver*)

Billy and Nell Sunday had established their household and reared their family of four children in Chicago for nearly twenty-three years when they decided to relocate their primary home to Winona Lake, Indiana. When one considers the decision, several insights into the Sundays' personal values come to light. Nell Sunday had lived her entire life in or near the Chicago area, and most of her large family remained there still in 1911. To many people, Billy Sunday was seen as the new evangelical Christian torchbearer, carrying on the work where nineteenth-century evangelist Dwight L. Moody left off. Given the influence of Moody on Sunday, reflected in the evidence in Sunday's library, it made perfect sense for Sunday to establish his ministry in Chicago where the Moody Bible Institute was located. Further, Chicago was a national hub of transportation, which suited Sunday's hectic travel schedule better than any other city in the Midwest. Lastly, by 1911 the Sundays had amassed a substantial sum of money and were certainly in a position to afford a new home in one of the many affluent Chicago suburbs. Despite all these logical reasons for the Sundays to remain in Chicago, they packed up their family of four children and moved to Winona Lake. What force could possibly have driven them to such an extreme change in lifestyle?

For almost fifteen years the Sunday family came to Winona Lake during the summer to enjoy the natural retreat environment and even bought a cottage there in 1900. While Billy Sunday annually participated in the Winona Bible Conference activities, he cherished his time at Winona, where he was free to be an average citizen and, if he desired, dress down in old clothes to do yard work (fig. 14). With the Sundays living largely out of trunks and suitcases from place to place, the family welcomed a slower pace during their breaks from the revival campaigns. Winona, with its vacationland atmosphere and convenient proximity to a major railway, provided an attractive retreat. The Sundays gave up the convenience of Chicago's metropolitan district and transportation hub in their backyard so that they might enjoy a wonderful sprawling park of a front yard with natural springs, tall oaks, and one of Indiana's finest lakes on the horizon. The Winona Christian Assembly's Bible Conference grounds, adjacent to the Sundays' bungalow, included these features as well as manicured flower beds, decorative fountains, swan ponds, and ornamental statuary of all kinds (fig. 35).

Ten years prior to the establishment of the Winona Christian Assembly's Bible Conference grounds in 1896, this same property was known to the public as Spring Fountain Park. The natural springs that feed into the lake from a steep bluff to the east provided the inspiration for a health spa resort, much in the same tradition as West Baden Springs, Indiana, or Hot Springs, Arkansas. Over the decade of 1885 to 1895, attractions were added, such as a switchback railway roller coaster, a horse track, a water slide, and a cyclorama — an oversized, round gallery that displayed a gigantic mural chronicling the battle of Lookout Mountain during the Civil War. By 1896 Spring Fountain Park was sold to the Winona Christian Assembly, whose first conference director just happened to be J. Wilbur Chapman, Sunday's old boss. Incidentally, once the Christian leaders took over the park grounds, the Lookout Mountain mural was painted over with a mural entitled "The Life of Christ" in the cyclorama. It's no wonder that the Sundays gladly traded the inconvenient one hundred miles to Chicago for this gated relaxing paradise in the bosom of nature and old friends.

The specific location of the Sunday's new home in the town of Winona also reflects their distinct family values. The first house that the Sundays owned in town was known as the Illinois, purchased in 1900 (fig. 36). The custom of naming one's home dated back to the Spring Fountain Park days and was a tradition the Sunday family wholeheartedly embraced. The Illinois, so named by the Sundays because they hailed from Chicago, was a Victorian-style lake cottage that sported decorative shingles and gingerbread as well as two stories of porches. At the urging of the Winona Christian Assembly's founder, Solomon Dickey, they bought the cottage complete with furnishings from a recently widowed preacher, a Dr. Lee, for the sum of $875.[1] Though the cottage was less than twenty-five years old when the Sundays decided to move to Winona permanently, it failed to suit their needs if it was to be used as a year-round residence. It had been built as a summer home and required refitting with a furnace and ventilation ducts as well as some means of insulation to weather the cold northern Indiana winters. Their full-scale relocation to Winona in 1911 gave Billy and Nell the opportunity to make their own statement by building a home to their specifications, something they had never attempted. While plenty of land was available for building on the east side of town, the Illinois lot commanded a prime location on the bluff overlooking the park

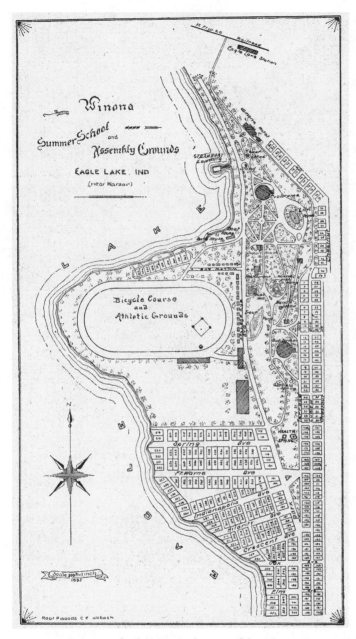

FIGURE 35. *Site map for the inaugural season of the Winona Summer School and Assembly Grounds (Winona Christian Assembly) in 1896. A few features from the Spring Fountain Park era of 1885–1895 carried over with new, more conservative functions, such as the horse track now renamed as the Bicycle Course and Athletic Grounds. Image courtesy of the Reneker Museum of Winona History, Grace College, Winona Lake, Indiana.*

FIGURE 36. *The Illinois, the first home that the Sunday family owned in Winona Lake circa 1908. Billy Jr., Paul, and George Sunday in foreground. In 1911 the Illinois was moved to the open lot behind so that the new Mount Hood bungalow could be built on the original site. Image courtesy of Joseph M. Sanford's* Billy Sunday: His Life as Seen through Picture Postcards, *2004.*

and lake and was just 500 feet from the Winona Auditorium, the central focus of the town. Instead of demolishing the Illinois, the Sundays decided to move the cottage to an adjacent lot, sell it, and build a new Arts and Crafts–style bungalow in its place.

The Mount Hood Bungalow

A house is built of bricks and stones, sills, posts, and piers;
but a home is built of loving deeds that stand a thousand years.
—Billy Sunday Speaks!

The new home that the Sundays commissioned from scratch is undoubtedly the single most important artifact in existence in providing

FIGURE 37. *Mount Hood bungalow circa 1925 after modifications were made,*
including the bay window in the dining room, a walk-in closet on the second floor,
and landscape improvements of the terraced garden, grape arbor pergola, and
cobblestone retaining walls. Image courtesy of Joseph M. Sanford's Billy Sunday:
His Life as Seen through Picture Postcards, 2004.

a useful material culture perspective on the Sunday family (fig. 37). The
home and its furnishings are in every way a reflection not only of the
Sundays' personal tastes but also of the times in which they lived. Upon
completion, the Sundays named their new bungalow Mount Hood, presumably a reference to the Hood River valley region of Oregon, where
the Sundays also owned a rustic cabin retreat and fruit orchard farm nes-
tled in the foothills of the real Mount Hood. Perhaps Winona Lake's
"Mount Hood" was the Sundays' way to bring a little piece of the Oregon
wilderness to northern Indiana.

Mount Hood, both from a purely architectural standpoint and through
the interior designs and furnishings placed in the home, is a prime example of the American Arts and Crafts style, also known in academic circles
as the Craftsman style or Mission Revival style. The Arts and Crafts
movement in America signaled a reform of values. The origins of the
movement began in mid-nineteenth-century England, largely as a reaction to the Industrial Revolution. The traditional ways of working, such
as learning a trade through an apprenticeship, hand-skilled workman-
ship, and journeyman status advancement, were being replaced by
mechanized mass-production of goods, task-specific specialization, and

a general devaluation of an individual worker's worth in the scheme of industrialized production. This shift in cultural values was evident to many in England, and several contemporary writers responded to these changes in their works. Charles Dickens's image of Ebenezer Scrooge in *A Christmas Carol* provides an excellent illustration, a personal copy of which belonged to the Sundays' youngest son, Paul. As a youth, prior to the era of heavy industrialization, Scrooge apprenticed with the family-owned Fezziwig Company, where he learned the craft and trade of the business over several years. In his late twenties, however, Scrooge abandoned Mr. Fezziwig so that he might manage his own business, which capitalized on the exploitation of workers. He also lost his fiancée when his desire for "Gain" outweighed any other pleasures or love of life.[2] Dickens's message was that "the machines, factories, and workhouses" represented a degradation of the human condition and thus required a regression to simpler times in order to turn the tide of humankind.

In the same manner, architects and theorists such as A. W. N. Pugin, John Ruskin, and William Morris reacted in less subtle ways. Pugin's *Contrasts* (1836) and *True Principles of Pointed or Christian Architecture* (1841) called for a return to the ethic of melding religion, art, and work into a common experience through the form of Gothic revival architecture.[3] In 1851 London's Great Exhibition of the Works of Industry of All Nations, the first world exposition of its kind, heralded the improvements of the modern era of industrialization by promoting mass-produced decorative works as equal or superior to traditional handcrafted works. Wasting no time in responding to this exposition, John Ruskin published his first volume of a series entitled *The Stones of Venice*, in which he berated the assumed benefits of an industrialized lifestyle.[4] For Ruskin, the Arts and Crafts movement involved more than a mere architectural style or interior design scheme. It was a value system based upon the four principles of design unity, joy in labor, individualism, and regionalism. The Sundays have in their library a beautiful leather-bound copy of Ruskin's 1862 work, *Unto This Last and Other Essays on Art and Political Economy*, which not only reflects Arts and Crafts axioms in its contents but is stylistically bound and laid out with Craftsman script and decoration (fig. 38).

While Ruskin led the charge philosophically as an academician, on the practical level no one surpassed William Morris in the application of the Arts and Crafts style. Morris, who called the overdone Victorian displays at the 1851 Great Exhibition "wonderfully ugly," brought handi-

FIGURE 38. *Clockwise from upper right: bungalow-style birdhouse, Rhodian Gouda water pitcher,* Unto This Last and Other Essays on Art and Political Economy, *Stellmacher pot, Nell Sunday's sewing basket,* Elbert Hubbard's Scrapbook, *throw pillow with embroidery by Nell Sunday. Items courtesy of the Billy Sunday Historic Site Museum, Winona Lake, Indiana.*

crafts to the forefront as a popular movement in England, culminating in the formation of the Arts and Crafts Exhibition Society in 1888.[5] William Morris put Ruskin's ideas to practical use and was best known as a designer of textiles and a manufacturer of textile dyes. Morris's influence is keenly felt in the numerous examples of decorative needlepoint completed by Nell Sunday (fig. 39). Nell's needlepoint and embroidery designs exhibit a flow of natural forms and shapes that are seemingly right out of a Morris design book.[6] Whether her pieces were used for practical applications, such as the covers for chairs or footstools, or purely as art pieces in the form of tapestry wall hangings, it is obvious that Nell Sunday internalized Morris's axiom, "There is no excuse for doing anything which is not strikingly beautiful."[7]

In America, the Arts and Crafts movement was never quite so intertwined with the political upheaval brought about by the Industrial Revolution as it was in England. Instead of being a rather expensive alternative to mass-produced goods as was the case in England, many patrons of the Craftsman style in the United States preferred it because

FIGURE 39. *The Sundays' master bedroom features needlepoint wall hanging and bench cover by Nell Sunday as well as Arts and Crafts decorative pieces such as the iridescent lamp and earthy umbrella stand. Image courtesy of the Billy Sunday Historic Site Museum, Winona Lake, Indiana.*

it used economical construction techniques and local building materials. Thus it became known as the "blue-collar architecture" of the early twentieth century. Key aspects of the Arts and Crafts movement in America were the emphasis on simplicity of design, handmade crafts, a blending with the natural environment, and a general humility of lifestyle. The Sundays' selection of this style for the only home they ever had built for themselves validates the interpretation that from an outward appearance, they espoused an antimaterialist view of life.

Architecturally, Mount Hood falls squarely into the building type known as the bungalow. With its exposed frame timbers and rafter tails, unadorned gables, and wide porches, the bungalow was the epitome of the Arts and Crafts home in America. On the inside, bungalows severely broke with the tradition of small rooms for specific functions, such as the vestibule, reception room, parlor, library, den, and music room of the Victorian home, and reintroduced the old notion of a "great room," or oversized living room, which could serve a multitude of functions in a more efficient manner. Gustav Stickley, a leader of the Arts and Crafts movement in America, wrote of the bungalow: "Here is a dwelling which embodies the essence of the Arts and Crafts philosophy. It is a house reduced to its simplest form where life can be carried on with the greatest amount of freedom. It never fails to harmonize with its surroundings. It is never expensive because it is built of local materials and labor; and it is beautiful as it is planned to meet the simplest needs in the simplest way."[8] These ideals struck a chord with the Sundays to such a degree that the family even desired that the wild birds live the simple life in a bungalow-style birdhouse made by Dodson Birdhouse Company (fig. 38).

One of the chief assets of bungalow architecture was its flexibility. Most bungalows featured a broad, sloping roof to the front of the house, with the gables running the length of the sides. The broad roof often created a large overhang in the front, allowing for a sizable front porch. However, with the lot shapes in Winona running narrow and deep, the Sundays were forced to design a bungalow with the exposed gables creating the overhang for the front porch and the broad, sloping roof running the length of the sides (fig. 40). The southern exposure along this long side employed banded windows to make the best use of natural light. These windows, which wrapped around to the west porch, provided the Sundays with an unbroken vista of the surrounding landscape. Nature was pulled right into the Sundays' laps through the use of this method. During the daytime, the view offered by the banded windows allowed the Sundays to watch birds, survey the floral gardens, and observe other flora and fauna. As time passed, the entire west end of the house became covered with climbing ivy, further emphasizing intimacy with nature. At night, however, these windows presented the problem of inadequate privacy, with the Sundays feeling as though they were living in a fish bowl. This obstacle was alleviated through the generous application of shades, curtains, and valances. In fact, in many windows, two rods were installed to allow for layering of window treatments.

The three porches, one open porch on the first floor and two enclosed sleeping porches on the second floor, also brought the outdoors into the everyday living environment. Porches, an integral element of bungalow architecture, exemplified the Sundays' closeness with nature, especially the sleeping porch. Sleeping porches, similar in function to a contemporary three-season porch, were usually built off upper-level bedrooms so that occupants could take advantage of the natural surroundings in an intimate setting. At Mount Hood, a small sleeping porch was off the

FIGURE 40. *South facade of Mount Hood bungalow showing details of shed dormer construction, exposed rafter tails, banded window design, and landscape improvements circa 1925. Image courtesy of the Reneker Museum of Winona History, Grace College, Winona Lake, Indiana.*

boys' bedroom, and a rather large one was directly off of the study, both on the second floor. For these sleeping porches, the Sundays cleverly employed a negative color scheme to the exterior of the home, with the walls and ceiling an earthy, semi-opaque, pea-green stain and the trim to windows and doors a dark-chocolate-brown-stained cedar. This color combination is precisely the opposite of the color scheme for the home's exterior, with the brown-stained cedar siding accented by pea-green window sashes. This reversal of color patterning cannot be construed as any type of accident. The porches and the exterior are the only places in the entire home that utilize these two colors, and it is obvious to even the casual observer that the earth-toned brown and green highlight a space specifically set aside for communing with nature. Overseeing all interior designs of the home, Nell Sunday was clearly, yet subtly, stating her awareness of the purpose that these rooms served and the vital role they played in everyday life.

With the exception of one room, the original color palette used at Mount Hood is entirely consistent with colors traditionally associated with the Arts and Crafts movement. Earth tones dominate this palette, with dark chocolate brown, forest green, raffia gold, iron rust, pea green, corn-husk yellow, and peanut shell tan. Only one room in the home stood out as being decorated with a color outside this Arts and Crafts palette — the bedroom for the two youngest boys, Billy Jr. and Paul. A brilliant scarlet red adorned the walls of this room, along with the oft-used peanut shell tan on the ceiling. These two boys were ten and four, respectively, when the home was built in 1911. While the color scheme in this room was in stark contrast to the colors seen elsewhere in the home, the bright red was perfectly appropriate for a room occupied by two young boys. Perhaps Nell succumbed to the wishes of her two youngest children, who might have wanted their place in the new house to be playful and happy instead of subdued and natural.

Beyond the mere physical architecture of the bungalow and the color palette, Mount Hood's interior design contained several splendid examples of the Arts and Crafts movement. Built-in furnishings, such as bedroom closets, library bookcases, the butler's pantry cupboard and countertop, and the inglenook in the living room, revealed the rigid control of the designer's intent for the space's use. The inglenook, a Swedish term that literally means "cozy place by the fire," comprised built-in benches flanking the fireplace, thus forcing the occupants to use the area in a specifically prescribed manner (fig. 41). Reportedly Nell Sunday's favorite place in the home, the inglenook was the site of many momentous events in the family's history, such as their daughter's engagement proposal.[9] Burlap wall treatments covered the walls in the living room, dining room, and below the chair rail in the halls and stairways. The burlap was treated with multiple layers of varnish and pigments to obtain a blotchy, organic texture that blends various hues of brown, gold, rust, and green. The stencil patterns on the burlap suggest a compromise between the ultrafloral expressions of the Art Nouveau movement and the strict geometric designs associated with other Arts and Crafts designers such as Frank Lloyd Wright. The stencil patterns in the upstairs bedrooms and study, like the ones on the first floor, indicate a simplicity in design while at the same time reflecting an appreciation of nature. Most extraordinary of the wall applications is a hand-painted seascape mural in the bathroom on the second floor. Painted by an unknown artist, the seascape includes the image of a lighthouse on a rocky shore, a metaphor often used to represent Christ, salvation, and hope.

While the use of earth-toned colors in the high-profile public areas and the porches was carried out in superb fashion at Mount Hood, such use of color in the public spaces was common for an Arts and Crafts home. Much more unusual, however, was the employment of the natural color

FIGURE 41. *The interior of the Mount Hood bungalow circa 1922 showing the inglenook with fire burning in the hearth. The mantle clock was a wedding gift from the Pittsburgh Allegheny ball club. Image courtesy of the William and Helen Sunday Archives, Grace College, Winona Lake, Indiana.*

palette in the service areas of the Sundays' home. Typically, service areas such as kitchens, pantries, laundries, and servants' quarters were finished with much simpler, inexpensive techniques because these spaces were not meant to be seen by guests. An Arts and Crafts home exhibiting naturalistic wall treatments and stencil designs in the public areas very often would have a plain white kitchen, a cultural phenomenon exemplifying antiseptic cleanliness as part of the modern technological improvements of indoor plumbing and gas cooking. Yet the walls and ceilings of the kitchen and butler's pantry at Mount Hood were origi-

FIGURE 42. *The "Stickley green" kitchen in the Mount Hood bungalow was designed to be a special treat meant only for the family's eyes. Image courtesy of the Billy Sunday Historic Site Museum, Winona Lake, Indiana.*

nally painted a dark forest green, and the pine woodwork in these areas was stained a rich translucent green (fig. 42). The kitchen and pantry doors, built-in cupboards, and utensil cabinets make use of heavy burnished copper hardware for handle pulls, hinges, and latches. The green-stained woodwork coupled with copper hardware is an unmistakable hallmark of "Stickley green," a stylistic line of furniture pieces produced by Gustav Stickley. The extension of the sophisticated Stickley green style into these service areas tells us not only that Nell Sunday was well versed in the techniques of the latest designers but also that she wholeheartedly believed in the philosophy of the Arts and Crafts movement. There would be no logical reason to bear the expense of time, materials, and effort to elaborately decorate a kitchen and pantry that would not be seen by guests unless the family members themselves desired this style of decoration.

Several decorative art pieces in the home's collection also exhibit exemplary Craftsman style. Nell Sunday's wonderful needlepoint pieces, influenced by the work of William Morris, are perhaps the purest manifestation of the Arts and Crafts values in the home's collection. With these objects, the home owner and artisan became one. The largest of her needlepoints is a five-by-three-foot wall hanging in the dining room of a red macaw parrot on a floral background (fig. 1). The Sundays had a macaw as a pet, and this 1927 wall hanging was likely a tribute to their beloved pet. Several of Nell's needlepoints were used for purely utilitarian purposes. A navy blue, white, and pink onion vine design covers the seat and back to a chair. In fact, the covering of this chair with her craft was a gift from Nell to Billy (fig. 41).[10] Floral needlepoints cover two footstools, the seat of a side chair, and the insert top of an end table. The pattern of an urn with flowers adorns a fire screen that Nell made as a gift for her youngest son, Paul.[11] A stylized reindeer is the central motif to the cover for a small bench. Of all the needlepoints, however, one example far surpasses the others, both in technical skill and exhibition of Arts and Crafts significance. The large three-by-four-foot naturalistic forest scene wall hanging not only has exquisite detail with a broad variety of brown and green hues that highlight the features in the nature scene, but also the central figures of two deer are executed in petit-point, thus allowing for even greater detail (fig. 39).

Besides Nell's own works, the Sundays supported the Arts and Crafts movement by purchasing furnishings made by other artisans producing this style. Several naturalistic prints hung on the walls of the home. A Wallace Nutting colorized photograph of a nature scene served as a Christmas greeting card worthy of keeping well after the holidays from the Sundays' friends G. H. and C. H. Johnson. A large settle, similar in function to a sofa, and a massive library table complemented the living room. The settle and table are both made of solid quarter-sawn oak, a favorite construction material of Craftsman-style artisans preferred because of the rich "tiger stripe" pattern obtained in the grain. Stickley even published the method used to cut the wood to obtain the desired appearance.[12] Two free-standing bookcases from the study also exhibit elements of this style, the larger of the two having heavy brass hinge flanges in the shape of dragons' heads, while the smaller bookcase features a decorative heart-shaped hole at the top of the case. Other articles in the home with the heart theme include stencil designs in both the study and Helen Edith's bedroom as well as a set of dinner chimes in the dining room. The simple shape of the heart was widely used by Craftsman designers from Fulper Pottery Company to Roycroft Studios of New York.[13] Not surprisingly, the Sundays have a copy of *Elbert Hub-*

bard's Scrapbook, the famous founder of Roycroft Studios, in their library collection (fig. 38).

The Sundays purchased or received as gifts several art pottery pieces of this era made by Rookwood, Weller, Nyloak, Stellmacher, and Rhodian Gouda (fig. 38). Weller vases and wall pockets of the "woodcraft" or "silvertone" design accented the butler's pantry. Examples of Rookwood pottery include candlesticks, a large flower bowl complete with frog, and several small vases and bowls. Many of the Rookwood pieces bear an inscribed "X" on the base, indicating that they were flawed "factory seconds" and most likely purchased by Nell rather than given as gifts. A mottled brown and gold ceramic umbrella stand grooved with a dark patina finish gives the illusion of growing directly from the floor (fig. 39). Even utilitarian items, such as the seventy-two-piece set of dinner china by KT&K Company, a 120-piece set of dinner china by Smith-Phillips Company, and a twenty-seven-piece set of silver-plated flatware bear the influence of the Arts and Crafts style with stylized Japanese key designs, herons, birds of paradise, and geometric floral patterns.

Of all the decorative arts in the home, the lighting devices most dramatically demonstrate the Craftsman style. The glass globes covering the ceiling light fixtures in the living room and dining room exhibit severely geometric rectangle and diamond patterns and seem to have been influenced heavily by Frank Lloyd Wright. Several ceiling light fixtures and wall sconces make use of heavy rectangular link brass chains and feature etched glass or end-of-day glass shades typical of the era. A large four-bulb table lamp with end-of-day glass panels, similar in style to a Tiffany Company product, adorned the library table in the center of the living room. An unusually shaped cut-glass lamp with an oval dome shade, possibly produced by Warsaw Cut Glass Company, located just two miles from the Winona Lake home, joined other gifts of cut glass on the Sundays' sideboard in the dining room. A wrought-iron floor lamp with green patina application and a paper shade with geometric designs produces a cozy orange hue when illuminated. A striking milk-glass table lamp with iridescent green and mustard freehand designs was originally one element of a three-part set that included two matching vases, which were kept on the fireplace mantle. An iron table lamp decorated with painted green leaves and a pine cone finial was found in the Sundays' basement in storage and had presumably been used in one of the children's bedrooms on the second floor. Perhaps the most stunning example of the Arts and Crafts style in the home is a table lamp in the shape of a mushroom. The cocoa brown Rookwood base is topped with a Handel Company art glass shade that yields exquisite textural patterns when lit. Produced in 1918, the mushroom lamp was placed in several locations of the home over the years, but its original location was in the study on the second floor (fig. 43).

In addition to the rich interpretive materials found inside Mount Hood, the immediate surroundings of the outdoor landscape also provide many clues into the minds of the family. The lot on which Mount Hood rests slopes dramatically from the top of the bluff (overlooking the lake) down nearly forty feet to the park floor. Rising from the Winona Christian Assembly grounds park boundary approximately a third of the way up the hill is an imposing forty-step concrete staircase leading to the west side and "front door" of the house. This staircase is divided into two segments. The first twenty-five steps follow the hill's slope of an eight-inch rise for every four horizontal feet. The second segment is a much steeper set of fifteen steps rising off the hill up to the outside porch. This hill provided the Sundays with ample opportunities to develop the landscape in creative ways. A bank of perennial plantings extended down the length of the hill along the north property line, and several photographs in the home's collection show Sunday weeding and raking leaves to maintain this planting bed (fig. 14). Biographical accounts also mention his use of the yard rake and shovel seen in these photos, which still survive in the home's basement along with a host of other gardening tools.[14] The lack of a garage during this period of rapid expansion of automobile ownership is a rather clear indication that Billy Sunday was not consumed with outward material possessions. He was known to have the use of privately owned automobiles from various hosts during his revivals across the country, and oral history maintains that he enjoyed his driving experiences to the point of being considered a "lead foot," but the Sundays never owned their own automobile. Accounts abound from local residents attesting to fact that the Sundays relied exclusively upon friends and neighbors for rides to nearby Warsaw or other destinations not accessible by rail.

By far the most enterprising modification of the landscape was the terraced garden on the south side of the house. A design plan from Peterson Nursery in Chicago exhibits a three-terrace garden, with a substantial portion of the middle terrace covered by a large pergola extending from the south side of the house approximately thirty feet (fig. 44). Historic photographs also confirm a large bed of hollyhocks, concrete benches, shrubbery, and a statuary birdbath on the top terrace (fig. 45).

FIGURE 43. *The Sundays' study on the second floor of the Mount Hood bungalow boasts more examples of Nell Sunday's needle crafts, a landscape oil painting by Nell, a love seat settee where the couple courted in the 1880s, the mushroom lamp, and the little writing desk that was the center of all the revival operations. Image courtesy of the Billy Sunday Historic Site Museum, Winona Lake, Indiana.*

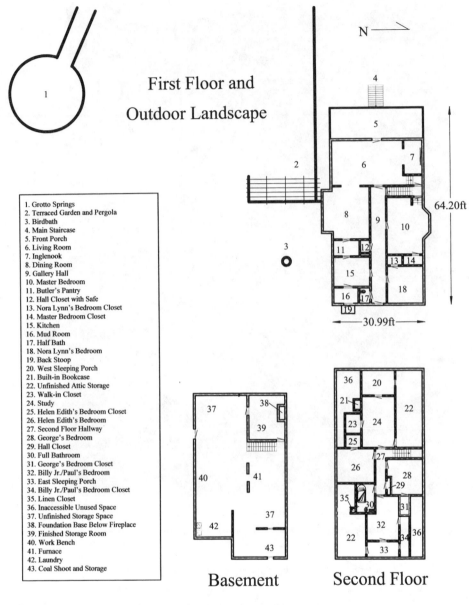

First Floor and
Outdoor Landscape

64.20ft

30.99ft

N

1. Grotto Springs
2. Terraced Garden and Pergola
3. Birdbath
4. Main Staircase
5. Front Porch
6. Living Room
7. Inglenook
8. Dining Room
9. Gallery Hall
10. Master Bedroom
11. Butler's Pantry
12. Hall Closet with Safe
13. Nora Lynn's Bedroom Closet
14. Master Bedroom Closet
15. Kitchen
16. Mud Room
17. Half Bath
18. Nora Lynn's Bedroom
19. Back Stoop
20. West Sleeping Porch
21. Built-in Bookcase
22. Unfinished Attic Storage
23. Walk-in Closet
24. Study
25. Helen Edith's Bedroom Closet
26. Helen Edith's Bedroom
27. Second Floor Hallway
28. George's Bedroom
29. Hall Closet
30. Full Bathroom
31. George's Bedroom Closet
32. Billy Jr./Paul's Bedroom
33. East Sleeping Porch
34. Billy Jr./Paul's Bedroom Closet
35. Linen Closet
36. Inaccessible Unused Space
37. Unfinished Storage Space
38. Foundation Base Below Fireplace
39. Finished Storage Room
40. Work Bench
41. Furnace
42. Laundry
43. Coal Shoot and Storage

Basement

Second Floor

FIGURE 44. *Floor plans for all three levels of the*
Mount Hood bungalow, including site information.

FIGURE 45. *The terraced garden on the south side of Mount Hood circa 1925. Hollyhocks were a favorite flower. Image courtesy of the William and Helen Sunday Archives, Grace College, Winona Lake, Indiana.*

Farther to the south of the terraced garden is the grotto springs, a circular cobble and masonry structure that confined the flow of the town's largest natural spring, previously known as "mammoth spring." The grotto springs feature was originally built in the 1890s by the landowner adjacent to the Illinois. By the late 1920s, however, the Sunday family was maintaining and using the grotto springs, and at one point Nell even dammed the outlet of the free-flowing spring to create a pond in which she raised goldfish. The outdoor terrain was, for the Sundays, merely an extension of the home's interior. From the informal interior with natural textured burlap walls, through the open-air sleeping porches, onto the terraced landscape, the Sunday property functioned as a continuous spectrum of the natural environment.

Family Relationships

Going to church doesn't make a man a Christian any more than
going to a garage makes him an automobile.—Billy Sunday *(Lockerbie)*

Up to this point, I have focused on understanding Billy Sunday and his impact on American values through an examination of his possessions. The goal of this section is to shed light on his personal relationships with his nuclear family by using the same methods. Taking such an approach in developing conclusions about personal relationships can be problematic, since very few items accurately reflect the way one person feels about another. Fortunately, the nature of many artifacts and images in this collection assist greatly in overcoming this obstacle.

The most important artifact at the Sunday site that can help with this interpretation is the house itself. The plan of the rooms and pattern of the space usage bear silent witness to the values of the Sunday family. An interpretation of a family based upon the layout of the house is valid for any new home commissioned to be built. However, in the case of Mount Hood, we may take the interpretation a significant step further. According to one newspaper account, Billy stated that Nell designed and planned the home herself.[15] Such a revelation should not be too surprising since she regularly reviewed blueprints and site plans for the numerous tabernacles that were constructed across the country for the revivals. In an interview three years prior to her death, she matter-of-factly recalled the precise size of rooms, hallways, and floor coverings in Mount Hood, as if she were still sitting at the drafting table.[16] The fact that Nell Sunday actually had a direct hand in coordinating the living

FIGURE 46. *The Sunday family circa 1908. Left to right: George, Billy Jr., Billy, Mary Jane Cory Sunday Heizer Stowell, Paul, Nell, and Helen. Image courtesy of the William and Helen Sunday Archives, Grace College, Winona Lake, Indiana.*

space allows the observer of this artifact a unique opportunity to gain insights into her thoughts, values, and beliefs.

The floor plan of the home incorporates several features common to bungalow architecture and Arts and Crafts style (fig. 44). Open lines of sight from room to room through the use of half-wall dividers, instead of floor-to-ceiling walls, and exposed beam ceilings are two hallmarks of this style. Similarly, banded windows providing views of the surrounding landscape and the incorporation of sleeping porches on the second floor intentionally integrate nature into the everyday living patterns of the inhabitants. Beyond the incorporation of these Craftsman-style elements, the structure of the space also relays information about the Sundays. Typical for the era, there is a clear separation of public and private space. The home is not particularly grand in size — a total of about 2,500 square feet — and not intended for large-scale entertaining. Only 27 percent of the home's space is formal in decor; the remaining 73 percent contains private areas for family members or household maintenance. Yet the Sundays were certainly aware of the dictum for providing pleasing formal spaces in the living-room and dining-room areas, while keeping the purely functional spaces hidden away from guests' vantage points. Only these formal spaces merit expensive quarter-sawn oak woodwork and elaborate ceiling light fixtures with hand-painted pressed-glass shades. All other areas of the home, including Billy's study and the master bedroom, reveal inexpensive pine woodwork and standard brass light fixtures. The inclusion in the living room of an inglenook, however, suggests that even in the formal areas, Nell desired a sense of coziness and intimacy.

Perhaps most telling is the layout of the family's sleeping quarters: two bedrooms on the first floor and three on the second. Predictably, the master bedroom, located on the first floor, is the largest of the bedrooms. But with the only full bathroom on the second floor, the layout creates the unusual situation of requiring Billy and Nell to climb the staircase to take a bath. By contrast, the children's bedrooms, all of which are on the second floor, provided prime access to that valuable commodity of indoor plumbing. A half bath on the first floor across the hall from the housekeeper's bedroom certainly eased the strain of this design, but it still seems unlikely that a master bedroom would be so far removed from the main bath. Perhaps it was this oversight that led to the renovation of the second-floor study nearly ten years after the home was built, so that it might serve as a master bedroom, and the old first-floor master bedroom was converted into the study. By the time of this switch, however, most of the children were grown and out of the home, so the precise interpretation of these changes remains laden with unknowns.

The room designated for the housekeeper and nanny, Nora Lynn, was logically located on the first floor near the kitchen and back door, areas where she would spend a great deal of time. Nora Lynn was for all practical purposes a member of the Sunday family (fig. 47). In the Sundays' employment for twenty years, she had a large hand in raising the children, especially Billy Jr. and Paul. She remained in the Sundays' employment

(opposite) FIGURE 47. *Nora Lynn in front of the Illinois circa 1912, the Sunday's first property in Winona Lake, shortly after it was moved to build Mount Hood. Nora Lynn remained in the Sundays' service until her death in 1930. Image courtesy of the William and Helen Sunday Archives, Grace College, Winona Lake, Indiana.*

until her death in 1930 at the Sunday home.[17] Curiously, her quarters were located the greatest distance possible from the children's bedrooms upstairs. The Sundays' master bedroom was somewhat closer to the children but still removed by a flight of stairs. There clearly existed a separation in living space between the children and the adults, which provides cause for speculation regarding the strained relationships between Billy and Nell and the Sunday children when they became adults.

Beyond the layout of the house and Billy's own anecdotes, a few personal artifacts also shed light on the relationships between the Sunday children and their parents. *Dear Old Father* and its companion, *Glorious Mother*, given by the author Samuel Francis Woolard in 1911 during the Wichita, Kansas, campaign, provide a nostalgic view of parenthood in the nineteenth century with which Billy and Nell identified. Further reinforcing these traditional values is *The Wedding Ring: A Series of Sermons on the Duties of the Husband and Wife* by T. DeWitt Talmage, which was a Christmas gift from Billy to Nell during the second year of their marriage (fig. 48). These texts espouse loyalty, trust, and the mutual commitment of husband and wife for the successful rearing of a family, all traditional ideals that Sunday stressed in his sermons.

However, Billy and Nell found the raising of their children much more difficult in practice than his sermons from the pulpit indicated. Helen Edith Sunday, the eldest of the Sunday children and their only daughter, was born on January 29, 1890, while Billy was still playing baseball. *The Human Body and How to Take Care of It* by James Johonnot and Eugene Bouton outlined the clean life for Helen and her brother George, who both read and used the book as children (fig. 48). All sources indicate that Helen lived this ideal lifestyle, but her health, ironically, became a great challenge. She attended DePauw University in Greencastle, Indiana, but had to withdraw on more than one occasion to battle a mysterious illness. Her fragile nature is well symbolized in her doll, which survived only through doting care (fig. 48). She moved with the family to Winona in 1911 but one year later married Mark P. Haines and set up housekeeping with him just across the Indiana state line in Sturgis, Michigan, where Haines was a newspaper publisher. Helen was continually afflicted by the recurring illness, which robbed her of strength and coordination. Undiagnosed at the time, it is likely that she had multiple sclerosis. She died on October 12, 1932, and was buried in Oaklawn Cemetery in Sturgis, at the family plot of her husband. Ironically, Helen, who was without question the closest of the Sunday chil-

FIGURE 48. *Clockwise from top center: Helen's doll,* Consolation, A Christmas Carol, Creative Chemistry, *George's tabletop clock, hot water bottle bed warmer, birthday gift tag from Billy Jr. to his father,* The Human Body and How to Take Care of It, In His Steps, The Destroyer, The Wedding Ring: A Series of Sermons on the Duties of the Husband and Wife. *Items courtesy of the Billy Sunday Historic Site Museum, Winona Lake, Indiana.*

dren to their parents, was the only one of the four not to be laid to rest next to Billy and Nell.

George Marquis Sunday, the eldest son, was born on November 12, 1892, while Billy was working for the YMCA. As a youth, George was given a 1903 edition of Charles M. Sheldon's *In His Steps* by his Sunday school teacher to help guide his path (fig. 48). George rose to the position of secretary in the Sunday organization during the height of Billy's popularity in the mid 1910s. He left the revival team at the close of 1917 to enlist in the war effort, where he was commissioned as a lieutenant in the aviation corps. After the war, however, temptation proved too strong for the Sundays' oldest son. He developed a taste for the luxuries of life and a lifestyle that included many of the vices that his father fought against: drinking, infidelity, multiple marriages, and theft. George's possession of a portable tabletop clock exemplifies his fast-paced life on the go in which time ran out too soon (fig. 48). He died in California on September 11, 1933, of complications from a fall off of a high-rise apartment building balcony. It was never concluded whether the fall was a murder, accident, or suicide, but the investigation determined that alcohol was a factor.

Billy Jr. and Paul grew up largely under the direct supervision of Nora Lynn, rather than their parents, who were both away from home seven to eight months of the year. William Ashley Sunday Jr., better known as Will or Billy Jr., was born on June 15, 1901. A novel he read as a youth, Burton E. Stevenson's *The Destroyer* (fig. 48), foretold his stormy relationships with his parents and future spouses. Billy Jr., who played piano for the Sunday revival team for a brief stint in the early 1920s, was frequently fawned over by his parents, who often remarked, "Will's the only good looking member of our family," referring to his piercing brown eyes. Eventually, however, Billy Jr. took after his older brother, George, and developed behaviors opposed to his parents' wishes, including heavy drinking and four unsuccessful marriages. As his father's namesake, Billy Jr.'s lifestyle during the Prohibition era of the 1920s was particularly embarrassing and disappointing to his father. Even so, Billy kept the handmade gift tag that Billy Jr. had attached to his father's birthday present in 1926 (fig. 48). Billy Jr. died on April 2, 1938, in a driving accident when he ran his car into a telephone pole returning home from an all-night party in Palm Springs, California.[18]

Paul Thompson Sunday was born on June 15, 1907, on his older brother Billy Jr.'s sixth birthday. Paul graduated from Warsaw High School in 1925, the only child of the Sundays to attend public high school, the other three all having attended private schools. Two of Paul's high school textbooks, *Creative Chemistry* (fig. 48) and *New Complete Geography — Indiana Edition*, bear witness to his own extracurricular activities. *Creative Chemistry* contains a letter Paul wrote to a classmate during a summer vacation in which he expressed his desire to get back with the old gang so that he could play poker, shoot dice, and play dominoes. He signed the letter "Saloon Paul." On the inside cover of Paul's geography textbook, he even wrote a poem that included the lines, "Give me a beer, Me for a whiskey, Oh joy! Wine." Perhaps it was this same zeal for merriment that led to his departure from his parents' teachings. Paul also had multiple marriages and tendencies toward the wild life of high-risk activities, dancing, and gambling. The last of the surviving Sunday children, Paul died in a military plane crash on February 24,

1944, while serving as a test pilot for Lockheed Aircraft Corporation during World War II. Paul's flight logbook in the family collection provides a glimpse into the activities of his last days.

The boys' behavior patterns became a factor leading either directly or indirectly to the untimely deaths of George in 1933 and Billy Jr. in 1938. With the additional deaths of Nora Lynn in 1930, Helen in 1932, George's son John in 1934, and Billy in 1935, the 1930s became an era of monumental change for the Sunday family. A number of books in the collection address this topic of death. A Bible given as a Christmas present in 1937 to Nell from Billy Jr., just a few months before his fatal auto accident, bears two inscriptions. The first reads, "To my darling mother with love and devotion, Your son, Bill." The second inscription in Nell Sunday's handwriting reads, "My darling left to be with the Lord April 2nd, 1938." Two books on grief, Mrs. Charles E. Cowman's *Consolation* (fig. 48) and *His Comfort: A Message of Help for Those Who Sorrow* by Norma B. Harrison, were gifts to Nell from friends concerned about her mental well-being during this stressful decade. These gifts of comfort, as well as hundreds of letters of support, served their purpose. Shortly after this wave of untimely deaths, Nell Sunday began her own tour of speaking engagements. She carried on the only way she knew how, strongly determined to let God lead her path. After Nell died on February 20, 1957, she was buried alongside Billy and the remains of their three boys in Forest Home Cemetery on the outskirts of Chicago. She had outlived everyone in the Mount Hood household.

Epilogue

*I would
rather have
standing
room in
heaven
than own
the world
and go to hell.*
—THE REAL
BILLY SUNDAY
(Brown)

Billy Sunday died of a heart attack at his brother-in-law's home in Chicago on November 6, 1935, just two weeks short of his seventy-third birthday. His last moments were tempered with the comfort of Nell's love, as she treated him to a bowl of Rice Krispies in milk and snuggled a hot water bottle at his feet (fig. 48). Only ten days prior to his death, he had delivered his final sermon to a packed church in Mishawaka, Indiana. Forty-one people responded to his last alter call, and on March 30, 2000, it was my privilege to interview Jane Powell Fesler, one of those converts from Sunday's last meeting. There is little question that Billy Sunday deeply touched the hearts and minds of his listeners from all backgrounds and of all ages. Her account of the event is poignant and succinct:

> Well, I was eleven years old. I went with the Brohmans, they had a daughter my age, and we were a close-knit group of friends. It must have been Sunday night that we went to hear Billy Sunday. He was a very forceful speaker, really touched my heart. I remember that he moved around quite a bit, and he was so fervent with his appeal. So when he made the alter call, I went forward and was prayed with there, which was just a very moving experience for me. After that, I sat down in the pew, and Mrs. Brohman put her arm around me. I remember her telling other people about the event—that I sat there and I was just trembling. But then suddenly, it was a peace that entered my heart. It has meant a lot to me, it was really a turning point in my life. . . . I know that Jesus is the answer to all things. The cliché that you see and hear, "Jesus saves," that's very true. Specifically, for our life here, and also the hereafter—where we're going to. I don't worry about what heaven looks like, whether the street's paved with gold, or a specific place. I just know that's what God has for us, and we don't want to miss that.[1]

An evaluation of Billy Sunday through material artifacts and images reveals a more complex person than the popular public perception. Supporters saw Sunday as a moral leader with few flaws. Perhaps South Bend, Indiana, industrialist Joseph D. Oliver summed up these thoughts best when he said, "There is nothing better in men than Billy Sunday himself, and few things worse than his imitators."[2] Sunday's critics saw a snake-oil-slinging charlatan, whose manipulation of the public turned ordinary citizens into brainwashed sheep. Noted poet Carl Sandburg concluded, "You, Billy Sunday, put a smut on every human blossom that comes in reach of your rotten breath belching about hell-fire and hiccuping about this man who lived a clean life in Galilee. . . . What the hell do you know about Jesus?"[3] Such flat interpretations, while entertaining, do a disservice to history because they present such narrow viewpoints and inadequate levels of detail.

Written accounts converge on Sunday's athleticism, conservative philosophy, charisma, and outspoken nature. The artifacts and images in the collection bear out this broad perception. Confirmation of his athletic achievements and physical fitness rests in his baseball equipment, gardening tools, and weight scales and in the numerous photographs of his physical manner of preaching. Sunday's library reflects a conservative philosophy and an ability to defend that stance through the use of empirical data. A few artifacts, however, may belie this conservative nature, most notably the brandy snifters, cordial glasses, and dance records. The multitude of gifts showered upon the Sundays speaks to his likability, not only during his heyday as an evangelist but also in his early days as a ballplayer and YMCA worker. Many of the gifts from his evangelistic days that carry some of his well-known epigrams validate his fiery, outspoken nature.

Criticisms of Billy Sunday in the written record include plagiarism, subversion of labor movements, perversion of Scripture, greed, and a lack of attention to his own family. The first count of plagiarism remains inconclusive at this point. The wholesale underlining of text from numerous volumes in the library collection provides a material foundation from which a thorough comparative analysis of Sunday's published sermons and these highlighted passages could be performed. No material evidence exists linking him to big business interests, aside from a few autographed photographs from business magnates of the era. In fact, some of the presentation gifts from the workers of the coal-mining districts in Pennsylvania and West Virginia suggest that Sunday was truly appreciated by the common laborer. No artifacts connect Sunday with a perversion of Scripture, but, admittedly, language patterns are a difficult field to represent materially. On the subject of greed, a preponderance of the evidence suggests that he was not affected by money. While it is true that very few people from the early twentieth century had two safes in their home, even fewer people with the wealth of Billy and Nell Sunday lived in a humble Arts and Crafts bungalow as a permanent residence and did not own an automobile. The austerity of Mount Hood and its contents speaks volumes about the values of the Sunday family. The layout of the home also suggests a clear separation between the parents and children, a segregation that may have resulted in strained relationships and perhaps contributed to tragically shortened lives for two of their children. The relationship between Billy and Nell, however, apparently was impregnable (fig. 49). Both were strong individuals who approached the challenge of life as a team sport, and both were so fully committed to the good of the team that at times each was blinded into making lamentable personal judgments.

One fact remains—whether it is showered with accolades or buried by criticisms, the Sunday name endures. During his own times, popular songs were written about Billy Sunday and his impact on American society, such as Al Jolson's comedy hit "When Sunday Comes to Town" written by Vincent Bryan and Harry von Tilzer, "Let's Stand by Billy Sunday" by Ernest R. Heck and F. E. Whitmore, "When Billy Sunday Comes to Town" by Joe Leaham and C. W. Bender, and "I Love My Billy Sunday but Oh You Saturday Night" by Edgar Leslie, Grant Clark, and George W. Mayer. Frank Sinatra reintroduced new generations to Billy Sunday, albeit in a negative light, in the hit "Chicago," written by Fred Fisher, when he reminded us that Chicago was "the town that Billy Sunday couldn't shut down." Sunday continues to this day to be a heroic figure for the Religious Right as well as a lightning rod for people sympathetic to past attitudes of intolerance, as witnessed in the unflattering portrayal of the Billy Sunday name in the 2000 movie *Men of Honor*. For better or for worse, it seems that Sunday refuses to go quietly into history.

As stated in the introduction to this work, artifacts do not reveal everything that happened in the past, but they very rarely lie about what they do tell us. According to the bulk of the surviving artifacts in their home at Winona Lake, the Sunday family lived a relatively modest lifestyle in a simple, inexpensive home. Billy Sunday was a real person with real talents as well as real challenges. As such, he made some deci-

FIGURE 49. *This 1925 photograph of Billy and Nell Sunday was taken inside their railroad car. The news wire picked up the image, and it ran in many papers across the country under the title "The Lovebirds." Image courtesy of the William and Helen Sunday Archives, Grace College, Winona Lake, Indiana.*

A Rosebud.

I would rather have a rosebud
  While I am here to see -
Than have the costliest flowers
  Placed on my coffin for me.

I would rather have a rosebud,
  A tribute of today -
Than have the richest laurels
  When I have passed away.

I would rather have a kindly smile
  From hearts forever true,
Than tears around my lifeless form
  When earth I've bade adieu.

I would rather have the kindest words
  That can be said to me,
Than flattered when my heart is still
  And life has ceased to be.

Then give me a rosebud sweet,
  A rosebud, pink, or red,
I'd rather have just one today,
  Than millions when I'm dead.

Henrietta Blair Heard

FIGURE 50. *This hand calligraphy and watercolor-tinted poem, "A Rosebud," by Henrietta Blair Heard, stresses enjoyment of life in the here and now, appreciation of nature and human relationships, and a general humility of lifestyle, themes consistent with the view of an intersection between the material and spiritual worlds. This framed poem has adorned the walls of Mount Hood since 1915.*

sions that raised the human spirit and some that left dreams unfulfilled. Sunday said it well at the twilight of his life when he stated: "We have the old sofa in our home on which we used to 'spark' and build our castles in the air, many of which have been crushed and lie in ruins at our feet, and some of which still stand, buttressed about by a love that blazes as brightly as it did when we plighted our eternal allegiance forty-three years ago."[4] The man who warned one hundred million people of hell-fire and shook the hands of nearly one million converts was not immune to the human condition.

Revivals and Appearances

No comprehensive list exists of Billy Sunday's revivals and speaking appearances. The information provided here is compiled from a variety of sources of both reasonable approximations as well as precise dates when known, so that a valid overall picture can be gleaned from the data. The work of compiling a comprehensive listing of all of Billy Sunday's revivals and isolated appearances is within our grasp, but it will take a large hand to accomplish the task. Known source materials spanning the country await a researcher's query, and the list provided below, while making use of over 200 sources, can only be considered a partial listing of Sunday's appearances.

This list of Sunday's 548 documented revivals and isolated appearances is arranged in alphabetical order according to state. For some revival campaigns, only a year is known; for many others, just the month(s) and year. A few fell so deeply through the cracks over the years that now we can only provide an educated guess at the date. Sadly, there are a few places where Billy Sunday reportedly spoke but no hint whatsoever exists to give even a reasonable estimation of the date. This last category runs dangerously close to hearsay, but these places have been included in this list in hopes of further substantiating the claims. The intermingling of precise figures with informed estimations can become misleading if the data are not strictly categorized according to their level of authenticity. For this reason, each entry is clearly labeled according to its documentary level of support. As old newspapers become indexed across the country, new information will certainly come to light. For the latest information on Billy Sunday's appearances, individuals should contact the Billy Sunday Historic Site Museum in Winona Lake, Indiana.

No marks accompanying figures utilizing the format "month/day/year–month/day/year" indicates fully documented information. Single-appearance dates are indicated by "month/day/year."

* = Either the beginning or ending date of the revival is unknown, shown in the format "month/day–month/day/year" or vice versa.

c = Year given is a reasonable approximation, plus or minus two years.

M = Month(s) and year documented.

P = Place-name of appearance location is the only known information; there is no date information.

S = Year is substantiated not with direct documentary evidence about the revival but by the fact that the sequence of this revival in the context of other documented revivals is known; hence the year shown is a reasonable assumption.

Y = Year documented.

United States

ALABAMA
Mobile   1–2/1927 M

ARKANSAS
El Dorado   1934 C

CALIFORNIA
Camp Kearny   10/27/1917 (during Los Angeles)

Los Angeles   9/2/1917–10/28/1917, 6/7/1925, 1/25/1931, 1934 Y

San Diego   8/7/1915–8/10/1915, 10/27/1917 (during Los Angeles), 1931 Y

Selma   1934 Y

COLORADO
Boulder   9/5/1909–10/10/1909, 7/16/1931

Canon City   3/26/1905–4/23/1905

Colorado Springs   6–7/1914 M

Denver   9/6/1914–10/25/1914, 4/7/1927, 4/30/1929

Salida   9/22/1906–10/21/1906

Sterling   5–6/1929 M

CONNECTICUT
Meriden   1935 Y
New Haven   3/16/1931–3/1931*

DELAWARE
Smyrna   1935 Y

FLORIDA
Daytona Beach   2/17/1921, 1931 Y, 1935 Y
Jacksonville   11/10/1920–12/20/1920
St. Augustine   3/1919 M
St. Petersburg   P
Tampa   3/20/1919–4/13/1919, 3–4/1927 M, 1935 Y
West Palm Beach   1931 Y

GEORGIA
Athens   11/24/1917 (during Atlanta)

Atlanta   11/4/1917–12/23/1917

Camp Gordon   11/29/1917 (during Atlanta), 12/19/1917 (during Atlanta)

Cartersville   12/10/1917 (during Atlanta)

College Park   11/17/1917 (during Atlanta)

Decatur   11/17/1917 (during
                  Atlanta)
Savannah   P
Toccoa   11/26/1917 (during
                  Atlanta)

ILLINOIS
Aledo   10/1905 M
Alton-Piasa   P
Aurora   4/10/1927–5/22/1927
Belleville   P
Belvidere   1901 C, 6/3/1902
Berwyn   1926 C
Bloomington   12/27/1908–2/3/1908,
                  4/1/1918 (during
                  Chicago)
Camp Epworth   10/1901 M
Canton   1905 Y
Carthage   1903 Y
Charleston   1908 Y, 8/1/1911
Chicago   10/25/1915,
                  3/10/1918–5/20/1918,
                  5/25/1930–5/31/1930,
                  1935 Y
Clinton-Weldon
    Springs   P
Danville   3/1910–4/16/1910*
Decatur   2/7/1908–3/17/1908,
                  1935 Y
Des Plaines   P
Dixon   2/16/1905–3/20/1905,
                  8/1932 M
Dundee   5–6/1900 M
Dwight   1907 Y
Elgin   11/1900 M
Eureka   7/5/1908
Farmington   1902 Y
Freeport   5/1906 M
Galesburg   9/28/1907–11/4/1907
Galva   3/18/1904–4/10/1904
Geneseo   P
Genoa   P
Gibson City   1907 S
Harvard   P
Harvey   1903 C
Havana   1908 Y

Hillsboro-
    Litchfield   1909 Y
Jacksonville   9/25/1908–11/5/1908
Kankakee   1907 Y
Kewanee   1906 S
LaGrange   1/13/1935
Lincoln   P
Lithic Springs–
    Shelbyville   P
Macomb   4/29/1905–5/28/1905
Marengo   3/1903 M
Moline–
    Rock Island   9–10/1919 M (same time
                  as Bettendorf–Davenport,
                  Iowa)
Monmouth   9/19/1926–10/1926*
Murphysboro   2/23/1907–3/1907*
Oneida   1898 Y
Pana   P
Peoria   10/1903 M,
                  5/20/1934–6/3/1934
Pontiac   11/5/1904–12/5/1904
Princeton   2/11/1906–3/17/1906
Prophetstown   6/10/1906–7/3/1906
Rantoul   9/1905 M
Richmond   P
Rockford   4/14/1904–5/1904*
Savannah   1897 C
Springfield   2/26/1909–4/1909*,
                  1934 Y, 1935 Y
Sterling   1898 Y,
                  2/11/1904–3/14/1904,
                  5/1927 M
Sycamore   8/25/1908
Walnut   6/25/1906 (during
                  Prophetstown)
West Frankfort   10/16/1927–11/27/1927
West Pullman   1903 C
Wheaton   5/1902 M
Woodstock   1902 S

INDIANA
Alexandria   7/31/1931
Anderson   5/23/1922 (during
                  Richmond)
Attica   P

Charleston-Salem	12/6/1897–12/26/1897
Elkhart	1914 Y
Evansville	1–2/1930 M, 1933 Y
Fairmount	3/30/1902–4/27/1902
Fort Wayne	1934 Y
Fountain Park–Remington	P
Hagerstown	5/26/1922 (during Richmond)
Hammond	P
Indianapolis	1935 Y
Lawrenceburg	1927 Y
Liberty	5/27/1922 (during Richmond)
Merom	P
Mishawaka	10/25/1935–10/27/1935
Nappanee	1934 Y
Petersburg	12/1927 M
Portland	5/17/1922 (during Richmond)
Richmond	1921 C, 4/16/1922–5/28/1922
Rochester	7/14/1908
Rockville	8/6/1911
South Bend	4/27/1913–6/15/1913
Spiceland	5/25/1922 (during Richmond)
Upland	1930 Y
Warsaw	P
Winchester	5/20/1922 (during Richmond)
Winona Lake	7/23/1911, 8/1912 M, 7/16/1916, 8/1916 M, 8/15/1919–8/21/1919, 8/13/1920–8/19/1920, 7/21/1921–7/24/1921, 7/5/1922–7/9/1922, 6/27/1924–6/29/1924, 7/6/1927, 8/23/1928, 8/1/1930, 8/9/1931, 8/17/1933, 7/29/1934, 8/4/1935

IOWA

Afton	3/6/1901–3/27/1901
Allerton	P
Alta	1897 Y
Ames	8/27/1926
Atlantic	2/1902 M
Audubon	1/1902 M
Bedford	1/1900 M
Bettendorf–Davenport	9–10/1919 M (same time as Moline–Rock Island, Illinois)
Bloomfield	P
Boone	1903 C
Burlington	11/9/1905–12/17/1905
Cedar Rapids	10/29/1909–11/21/1909
Centerville	1902 Y
Clarksville	1/27/1898–2/15/1898
Clear Lake	P
Corydon	10/1901 M
Council Bluffs	9–10/1915 M (during Omaha, Nebraska)
Des Moines	11/2/1914–12/20/1914, 10/31/1921, 3/1932 M, 1/15/1933–2/1933[*]
Dubuque	P
Dunlap	1897 C
Eddyville	P
Elliot	1897 C
Emerson	1896 C, 1899 C
Exira	9/18/1901–10/13/1901
Fairfield	1907 S
Garner	1/8/1896–1/15/1896
Glenwood	P
Grundy Center	1901 Y
Harlan	6/1901 M
Hawkeye	1898 C
Humboldt	1896 C
Iowa City	1910 Y
Jefferson	12/1903–1/3/1904[*]
Keokuk	10/5/1904–11/5/1904
Knoxville	1907 S
Leon	1901 S
Malvern	1899 C
Marshalltown	1909 Y
Mason City	1/1905 M
Mediapolis	P

Muscatine	11/10/1907–12/15/1907
Nevada	8/1926 M
New Hampton	1898 C
New Sharon	1896 C
Oakland	P
Oakville	1898 Y
Olin	P
Osceola	1902 Y
Oskaloosa	2/1/1896
Ottumwa	1896 C,
	11/6/1908–12/16/1908
Perry	1/1901 S
Seymour	12/23/1900–1/20/1901
Sibley	1897 C
Sigourney	1/19/1896–1/30/1896
Silver City	2/24/1897–3/9/1897
Sioux City	9–10/1921 M, 1934 Y
Tabor	1897 C
Wapello	P
Washington	P
Waterloo	11/7/1910–12/19/1910,
	11/1932 M
Webster	1/31/1896
West Union	7/1908 M
Williamsburg	1898 C

KANSAS

Coffeeville	9/15/1929–10/27/1929
Dodge City	11/3/1929–12/15/1929
Hutchinson	1930 C
Iola	3–4/1928 M
Witchita	11/12/1911–12/25/1911,
	2/1930 M

KENTUCKY

Carrollton	1923 C
High Bridge	P
Louisville	4/22/1923–5/1923 *
Madisonville	9/126/1928–10/27/1928

LOUISIANA

Shreveport	3–4/1924 M

MAINE

Bangor	5/29/1927–7/3/1927
Portland	6/6/1927

MARYLAND

Baltimore	2/28/1916–4/23/1916,
	1932 Y
Elkton	1932 Y
Glyndon	P
Mountain	
Lake Park	P
New Market	1933 Y

MASSACHUSETTS

Boston	11/12/1916–1/21/1917,
	6/20/1927 (during
	Bangor, Maine),
	2/17/1931–3/1/1931,
	1931 Y
New Bedford	1916 Y

MICHIGAN

Ann Arbor	10/1916 M (one day
	during Detroit)
Big Rapids	1934 Y
Bronson	P
Detroit	9/10/1916–11/5/1916,
	10/12/1927, 5/19/1930,
	9/7/1930, 10/11/1932,
	10/1934 M
Grand Rapids	11/6/1916 (during
	Detroit)
Manistee	P
Pontiac	5/31/1928
Sturgis	1916 M (one day during
	Detroit)

MINNESOTA

Austin	3/1906 M
Browns Valley	P
Buffalo	P
Duluth	5/26/1918–7/7/1918
Elmore	1905 C
Marshall	1–2/1904 M, 12/19/1904
	(during Redwood Falls)
Minneapolis	1934 Y
Moorehead	P
Paynesville	7/26/1931
Redwood Falls	12/10/1904–1/9/1905
Rochester	12/28/1905–1/29/1906
Sleepy Eye	1/10/1905

Wilmar P
Worthington 12/7/1906–1/13/1907

Jackson 12/28/1924–2/1/1925

MISSOURI
Cape Girardeau 3–4/1926 M, 12/1933 M
Chillicothe 1914 C
Joplin 12/12/1909–1/1910*
Kansas City 4/30/1916–6/18/1916,
12/17/1929, 1935 Y
Maryville 1899 C
St. Louis 1/15/1928–2/26/1928

MONTANA
Havre 1931 Y
Livingston 10/1931 M

NEBRASKA
Beatrice P
Fullerton P
Lincoln 1930 Y
Omaha 9/5/1915–10/24/1915
Pawnee 1896 Y
Tecumseh 1897 C

NEW JERSEY
Elizabeth 1934 Y
Lambertville 2/16/1915
Mt. Holly 4/13/1930–5/18/1930
Newark 1930 Y
Ocean Grove 8/31/1916, P
Paterson 3/27/1915–5/28/1915,
1934 Y
Pitman 8/1929 M
Princeton 1933
Trenton 1/1916–2/21/1916*
Vineland 1930 Y

NEW YORK
Binghamton 12/1922 M, 1/4/1926–
2/21/1926
Boonville P
Buffalo 1/28/1917–3/25/1917,
1931 Y, 1932 Y, 1933 Y
Elmira 9–10/1924 M
Hutchinson 11/9/1930–12/4/1930

Millbrook 1933 Y, 1934 Y, 1935 Y
New Haven-
Dempster
Grove P
New West
Brighton 1934 Y
New York City 3/9/1914, 4/8/1917–
6/19/1917, 1918 (one day
during Washington,
D.C.), 1/7/1934–1/21/1934
Niagara Falls 9–10/1923 M
Syracuse 10/31/1915–12/19/1915,
3/5/1920–3/14/1920

NORTH CAROLINA
Albemarle 2/6/1924 (during
Charlotte)
Charlotte 12/30/1923–2/10/1924,
5/18/1925 (during
Winston-Salem)
Concord 2/4/1924 (during
Charlotte)
Davidson 2/8/1924 (during
Charlotte)
Elkin 4/27/1925 (during
Winston-Salem)
Gastonia 1/11/1924 (during
Charlotte)
Greensboro 2/17/1919 (during
Richmond), 4/28/1925
(during Winston-Salem)
Greenville 5–6/1928 M
High Point 5/13/1925 (during
Winston-Salem)
Kannapolis 2/4/1924 (during
Charlotte)
Kernersville 5/28/1925 (during
Winston-Salem)
Lincolnton 1/29/1924 (during
Charlotte)
Mayodan 5/10/1925 (during
Winston-Salem)
Mount Airy 5/25/1925 (during
Winston-Salem)
Pilot Mountain 5/11/1925 (during
Winston-Salem)

Raleigh	6/2/1925
Reidsville	5/20/1925 (during Winston-Salem)
Salisbury	1/14/1924 (during Charlotte)
Spencer	1/14/1924 (during Charlotte)
Walnut Cove	5/10/1925 (during Winston-Salem)
Waxhaw	2/2/1924 (during Charlotte)
Wilmington	4/9/1923
Wilson	3/26/1923 (during Columbia, South Carolina)
Winston-Salem	4/19/1925–5/31/1925, 6/2/1925
Yadkinville	5/16/1925 (during Winston-Salem)

NORTH DAKOTA

| Devil's Lake– Lakewood Park | P |
| Fargo | 4/7/1912–5/12/1912 |

OHIO

Asland	1929 Y (during Elyria)
Bradford	5/4/1922 (during Richmond, Indiana)
Campbellstown	5/24/1922 (during Richmond, Indiana)
Canton	12/31/1911–2/11/1912, 11/1931 M
Celina	1910 C
Chautauqua- Franklin	8/11/1929
Cincinnati	3/6/1921–5/1/1921, P
Cleveland	2/23/1926, 1929 Y (during Elyria), 10/20/1930
Columbus	1/30/1911 (during Portsmouth), 12/29/1912–2/16/1913, 5/1913 M (one day during South Bend, Indiana), 1915 Y (one day during Philadelphia), 5/28/1923, 10/13/1930, 7/17/1935
Dayton	11–12/1922 M
Delaware	2/12/1913 (during Columbus)
Dunkirk	12/1912 M
East Liverpool	9/15/1912–10/27/1912, 11–12/1928 M
Elyria	1/13/1929–2/24/1929
Greenfield	P
Greenville	5/6/1922 (during Richmond, Indiana)
Ironton	1930 Y
Lakeside	8/18/1929, 8/17/1932
Lancaster	8/4/1929, 8/13/1929
Lima	2/19/1911–4/2/1911
Lorain	1929 Y (during Elyria)
Marysville	1/1913 M (one day during Columbus)
Middletown	7/14/1930
New Paris	5/19/1922 (during Richmond, Indiana)
Piqua	P
Portsmouth	1/1/1911–2/12/1911
Springfield	9/24/1911–11/5/1911
Steubenville	9/14/1913–10/26/1913
Toledo	4/9/1911–5/21/1911
Van Wert	1912 Y
Wellington	1929 Y (during Elyria)
Youngstown	1/2/1908, 1–2/1910 M, 1932 Y

OKLAHOMA

| Oklahoma City | 5–6/1920 M |
| Tulsa | 11–12/1921 M |

OREGON

Gladstone	P
Pendleton	1919 Y
Portland	9/6/1925–10/1925*, 1933 Y, 1934 Y

PENNSYLVANIA

| Altoona | 1932 Y |
| Beaver Falls | 5/16/1912–6/24/1912 |

Erie   5/28/1911–7/9/1911, 1929 Y (during Elyria, Ohio) 10/22/1933–10/30/1933

Franklin   3/1931–3/15/1931*, 1932 Y

Harrisburg   1931 Y, 1932 Y

Johnstown   11/2/1913–12/14/1913, 1932 Y

Lancaster   1930 Y

McKeesport   11/3/1912–12/14/1912

New Castle   9/18/1910–10/31/1910

Penn Grove   P

Philadelphia   1904 Y, 3/14/1914 (during Scranton), 1/3/1915–3/20/1915, 2/14/1916, 4/10/1922, 3/1930 M, 1933 Y

Pittsburgh   12/28/1913–2/23/1914, 1932 Y

Scranton   3/1/1914–4/20/1914

Shamokin   1932 Y

Sharon   5–6/1908 M

Wilkes-Barre   2/23/1913–4/13/1913, 1/30/1926

Williamsport   10/1913 M, 11–12/1925 M

RHODE ISLAND

Newport   11/1918 M

Providence   9/22/1918–11/3/1918

SOUTH CAROLINA

Camden   3/21/1923 (during Columbia)

Charleston   11/4/1923–12/16/1923

Clinton   3/5/1923 (during Columbia)

Clover   1/19/1924 (during Charlotte)

Columbia   2/25/1923–4/8/1923

Florence   3/27/1923 (during Columbia)

Marion   4/9/1923

Newberry   3/24/1923 (during Columbia)

Orangeburg   3/12/1923 (during Columbia)

Spartanburg   1–2/1922 M, 1/21/1924 (during Charlotte, North Carolina)

Sumter   3/19/1923 (during Columbia)

York   1/19/1924 (during Charlotte, North Carolina)

SOUTH DAKOTA

Sioux Falls   1934 Y

TENNESSEE

Bristol, Tennessee- Virginia   3/21/1920–4/1920*

Chattanooga   11/9/1919–12/21/1919, 4/10/1923, 12/1/1924 (during Nashville), 1931 Y, 4/28/1935–5/18/1935

Cleveland   4/22/1935–4/26/1935

Knoxville   1/7/1923–2/18/1923, 4/10/1935–4/21/1935

Maryville   1923 C

Memphis   5/1924 M, 2/1925 M, 1926 Y, 10/24/1928, 12/28/1931

Morristown   6/4/1922–6/1922*

Nashville   11–12/1924 M

TEXAS

Corpus Christi   3–4/1929 M

Fort Worth   11–12/1918 M, 1930 Y

Houston   1934 Y

VIRGINIA

Bristol, Tennessee- Virginia   3/21/1920–4/1920*

Camp Lee   1/20/1919 (during Richmond)

Danville   10/9/1922 (during Lynchburg), 1925 Y

Harrisburg   P

Lynchburg   9–10/1922 M, 6/1/1925

Newport News   3–4/1925 M

Norfolk-
Portsmouth 1/4/1920–2/29/1920
Norton 6–7/1921 M
Petersburg 11/21/1919 (during
Richmond), 2/26/1919
(during Richmond)
Quantico 2/10/1919 (during
Richmond)
Richmond 1/12/1919–3/2/1919
Roanoke 9/19/1920–10/31/1920,
5/21/1921, 10/30/1928
Staunton 5–6/1926 M
Wilder P

WASHINGTON
Bellingham 4/23/1910–5/29/1910
Everett 1910 Y
Olympia P
Seattle P
Spokane 12/25/1908–2/1909*
Vancouver P
Yakima 11–12/1926 M

WASHINGTON, D.C.
1/6/1918–3/3/1918,
4/7/1931

WEST VIRGINIA
Beckley 6–7/1923 M
Bluefield 5/8/1921–6/1921*
Charleston 3/1922–4/9/1922*,
1930 Y
Fairmont 11/1912 M, 1–2/1921 M
Huntington 4/28/1914–6/1914*,
1930 Y
Logan 5–6/1923 M
Wheeling 2/18/1912–3/31/1912,
1/12/1914 (during
Pittsburgh), 1933 Y

WISCONSIN
Belleville P

Canada

ONTARIO
Toronto 11/22/1914

Appendix B
Conversions

This list of Sunday's 870,075 documented converts from 1896 to 1935 is arranged by month and year in order to demonstrate clearly the pattern of his impact and public influence. Sunday averaged 7,312 converts per revival for these revivals; however, this list is far from complete. Nearly 78 percent of the places listed in appendix A are not represented in this table of conversions. For several of the revivals, estimations of conversions were made by local newspapers or other organizations when a precise head count was not taken, and for the sake of providing as much data as possible, these figures have been included with appropriate designations. In many instances, sources conflicted over precise numbers; however, in all circumstances, the most specific information available from the most reliable source is the figure presented. No attempt has been made to estimate conversion figures for revivals with no previous conversion estimates.

It is especially unfortunate that documentary evidence for conversion figures begins to dramatically fall by the wayside in 1918, just as Sunday began a new pattern of leading revivals extensively in the South. After 1918, he was admittedly past his peak, but Sunday was still a formidable force, leading another fifty-six campaigns of more than one month in length during the 1920s. For example, on April 8, 1923, the closing day of his revival in Columbia, South Carolina, he had 4,440 converts, the second largest single-day convert count in his career, behind only the final day total of 7,436 converts during the New York City revival in 1917. It seems likely that Sunday's lifetime total for converts is significantly higher than the 1,000,000 mark approximated by several other Sunday biographers. While 1,000,000 is an easy number to remember, it is perhaps short by as many as 250,000.

\# = Estimate calculated by local newspaper or other organization.

\+ = Revival began in previous year and concluded in the year shown.

* = Indicates a discrepancy between two or more different sources. Specific numbers are given precedence over estimates; however, in the case of all factors being equal, the most conservative number is shown.

1896			
Garner IA	268		

1897	
Charleston-Salem IN	200
Emerson IA	100#
Sibley IA	250#
Savannah IA	200#

1898	
Clarksville IA	125

1899	
Emerson IA	100#
Malvern IA	230

1900	
Bedford IA	388*
Elgin IL	725

1901	
Seymour IA+	400#
Afton IA	300#
Corydon IA	413

1902	
Atlantic IA	565
Fairmount IN	607
Wheaton IL	250
Belvidere IL	520
Centerville IA	900#
Woodstock IL	350

1903	
Marengo IL	500#
Harvey IL	400#
West Pullman IL	600#

Boone IA	500#
Carthage IL	427

1904	
Jefferson IA	516
Marshall MN	620
Sterling IL	1,652*
Galva IL	618
Rockford IL	1,000#
Keokuk IA	900#*
Pontiac IL	1,054*

1905	
Redwood Falls MN+	591*
Mason City IA	1,000#*
Dixon IL	1,354*
Canon City CO	934*
Macomb IL	1,880*
Canton IL	1,120
Rantoul IL	550
Aledo IL	974
Burlington IA	2,484*

1906	
Rochester MN+	1,244*
Princeton IL	2,225*
Austin MN	1,387*
Freeport IL	1,365*
Prophetstown IL	900#
Salida CO	612*
Kewanee IL	3,018*

1907	
Worthington MN+	1,037
Kankakee IL	2,650

Murphysboro IL	2,180	Fargo ND	3,159*
Fairfield IA	1,118	Beaver Falls PA	4,229*
Knoxville IA	1,017	East Liverpool OH	6,354
Gibson City IL	1,000#	McKeesport PA	10,022
Galesburg IL	2,508*		
Muscatine IA	3,579	**1913**	
		Columbus OH+	18,333*
1908		Wilkes Barre PA	16,548*
Bloomington IL+	3,865*	South Bend IN	6,098*
Decatur IL	6,209*	Steubenville OH	7,888
Charleston IL	2,467	Johnstown PA	11,829
Sharon PA	4,731		
Jacksonville IL	3,002*	**1914**	
Ottumwa IA	3,732	Pittsburgh PA+	25,797*
		Scranton PA	16,999*
1909		Huntington WV	5,812
Spokane WA+	5,666*	Colorado Springs CO	4,288
Springfield IL	4,729*	Denver CO	8,100#
Marshalltown IA	2,026	Des Moines IA	10,200#
Boulder CO	1,347*		
Cedar Rapids IA	2,906	**1915**	
		Philadelphia PA	39,331*
1910		Paterson NJ	14,386*
Youngstown OH	5,965*	Omaha NE	13,022*
Danville IL	5,000#	Syracuse NY	21,155*
Bellingham WA	4,500#		
Everett WA	4,000#	**1916**	
New Castle PA	6,683	Trenton NJ	19,640
Waterloo IA	4,500#	Baltimore MD	23,085*
		Kansas City MO	20,646*
1911		Detroit MI	26,911
Portsmouth OH	5,224*		
Lima OH	5,659*	**1917**	
Toledo OH	7,686	Boston MA+	63,484*
Erie PA	5,314*	Buffalo NY	38,853
Springfield OH	6,804*	New York City NY	98,264
Wichita KS	5,245*	Los Angeles CA	26,752
		Atlanta GA	14,715
1912			
Canton OH+	5,654*	**1918**	
Wheeling WV	8,437*	Chicago IL	49,165
		Providence RI	10,119

1919		1924	
Richmond VA	6,000#	Charlotte NC	7,765
Tampa FL	5,500#		
		1926	
1921		Cape Girardeau MO	1,319
Cincinnati OH	15,000#		
		1929	
1922		Elyria OH	3,500#
Richmond IN	4,777		
		1935	
1923		Mishawaka IN	42
Columbia SC	17,232		

Appendix C
Evangelistic Team Members

As was the case with the revivals and conversions, some facts have been lost over the years with regard to Billy Sunday's evangelistic team members. The list below is a compilation of documented team members, along with functional roles and years of service when known.

NAME	FUNCTIONAL ROLES	YEARS OF SERVICE
B. D. Ackley	private secretary, pianist, staff writer, public relations manager	1907–1915
Homer Alexander	Bible study teacher	1904
Edith Anderson (Butler)	vocalist	1909
Virginia Asher	director of extension work, director of business women's work, vocalist	1911–1927
William Asher	Bible study teacher, advance agent	1911–1921
G. Walter Barr	staff writer	ca. 1905–1908
Paul Beckwith	pianist, staff assistant	1925–1926
George Ashley Brewster	pianist, vocalist	1916–1919
Elijah P. Brown	authorized biographer, staff writer	1906–1907, 1912–1913
Charles Butler	vocalist, musical assistant	1907–1909
William Butterfield	tabernacle custodian	1918–1919
John Cardiff	masseur, physical trainer	1912–1917
Harry Clarke	song leader, general organizer	1932–1935
William Collison	staff assistant	1913
Mrs. Connett	vocalist	1905
Otis G. Dale	business manager	1918
George G. Dowey	director of men's Bible study	ca. 1915–1918
Rev. Ed Emmet	advance agent	1914
Rose M. Fetterolf	high school work, assistant women's work	1916–1917
Fred Fischer	song leader	1900–1910
Mrs. Fred Fischer	vocalist	1904–1907
Miss Franchere	violinist	1905
Rev. J. Glenn Frank	staff assistant	1909

Alice Gamlin	director of boys' and girls' work	1916–1917
Albert Price Gill	tabernacle architect, advance agent	1908–1912
Mrs. Albert Price Gill	role unknown	1908–1912
Homer Hammontree	choir director	1927–1929
Mr. Harper	role unknown	1907
Mrs. Harper	role unknown	1907
Willis Haymaker	advance agent	1930
I. E. Honeywell	private secretary, assistant evangelist	1904–1917
Walter Jenkins	interim choir director	1923–1925
James "Uncle Jimmy" Johnson	staff assistant	1912
Wade Hampton Johnson	volunteer trainer	1915
Howard A. Johnston	volunteer trainer	ca. 1915–1918
Florence Kinney	director of student work, director of business women's work, pianist, Bible study teacher	1916–1930
Jean Lamont	assistant Bible study teacher	1916–1917
Hugh Laughlin	song leader	1912
John Linden	staff assistant, director of men's work	1909–1918
Willis Locke	tabernacle custodian	1929–1930
Mamie Lorimer	vocalist	1901–1902
A. B. MacDonald	men's work assistant	1917
Anna MacLaren	vocalist	1909–1916
Robert Matthews	pianist, private secretary	1916–1930
Frances Miller	Bible study teacher, director of business women's work	1906–1917
Rae Muirhead	Bible study assistant	1908–1910
French Oliver	song leader, advance agent	1897–1898
Rev. L. K. Peacock	assistant evangelist, general campaign manager	1911–1915
Albert Peterson	tabernacle custodian, advance agent, masseur	1915–1930
Roy Peterson	tabernacle custodian	1927
Harland H. Pitzer	campaign manager, director of Bible study	1918–1920

Clifton Pryor Pledger	assistant evangelist	1908–1909
Miss Poxen	women's activity director	1905
Fred W. Rapp	advance agent, business manager	1920–1924
Homer Rodeheaver	song leader, choir director	1908–1928
Ruth Rodeheaver	vocalist	1920
Alvin W. Roper	pianist	1918
Robert Morrill Sand	advance agent	ca. 1925
Grace Saxe	Bible study teacher	1911–1921
Fred Seibert	staff assistant, tabernacle custodian	1898, 1905–1915
Joseph Spiece	tabernacle custodian, building supervisor, advance agent	1906–1918
Dena P. Stover	assistant student worker, women's worker, cornet soloist, vocalist	1914, 1922–1923
George M. Sunday	private secretary, business manager	1912–1918
Helen A. Sunday	business manager	1908–1935
William A. Sunday Jr.	pianist	ca. 1922
Melvin Trotter	staff assistant	1907–1909
J. R. Van Winkle	song leader	1896
James E. Walker	advance agent	1916–1919
Isaac Ward	director of men's work, shop work supervisor	1916–1917
John Wallace Welsh	advance agent	1916
Florence K. Whitbeck	reservations secretary	1917–1918

Appendix D
Family Genealogy

Genealogical research is in many ways similar to peeling an onion—with each freshly uncovered layer, there is a new reason to cry. With the circle of family history research growing wider every day, it is quite likely that many kin relationships to Billy Sunday or his wife, Helen Thompson, will surface after publication of this work. The goal of this genealogy is to show the overall structure of Billy Sunday's family, not necessarily to achieve an exhaustive family tree. The assembly of a total family-tree diagram, while interesting, would be too unwieldy for the format of this book; therefore, an hourglass-style diagram has been employed to provide a concise picture of the core structure of his family. The subsequent kinship report offers the names of a myriad of Sunday relatives, most of whom were discovered as a result of this study, along with their birth dates when known and their relationship to Billy Sunday. To obtain current genealogical information on the Sunday and Thompson families, contact the Billy Sunday Historic Site Museum in Winona Lake, Indiana.

The most often asked question pertaining to the Sunday family is, "Are there any surviving descendants of Billy Sunday?" After months of research focused on this specific question, the answer regrettably remains, "We're not absolutely sure." Billy Sunday had only three grandchildren: John M. Sunday, who died as a teenager in automobile accident in 1934; Mark Paul Haines, who died at the age of thirty-nine of acute hepatitis, only a few months after his grandmother Nell Sunday died while visiting him in Phoenix; and George Marquis Sunday Jr., who died in 1968. Of these grandchildren, only George Jr. had children, one boy, Marquis Ashley Sunday, Billy Sunday's only known great-grandchild. Marquis, known as Marq, was born in Los Angles on September 15, 1940, shortly after which his parents separated and Marq was left without the care of either parent. His mother, Alma Baine, attempted to gain custody rights in 1947 but lost the case, leaving Marq to be reared by his grandmother, Harriet Mason Sunday. After Harriet died in 1960, Marquis slipped away from view until his violent death in San Francisco on March 22, 1982, at the age of forty-one. Marquis was shot in the chest with a .22-caliber pistol during an argument with his common-law wife, Barbara Barnato. To date, no obituary, Social Security record, or other document of any kind has been found to determine if Marquis Sunday had offspring.

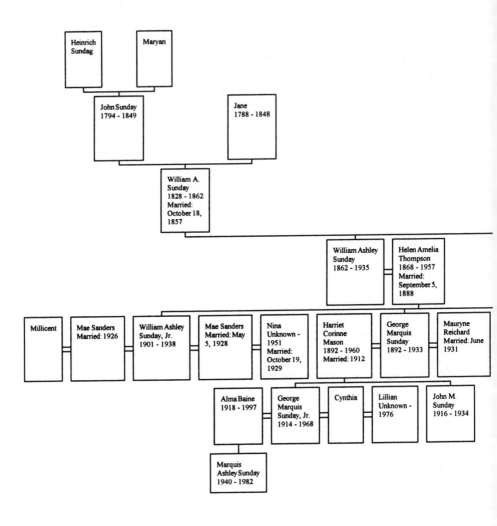

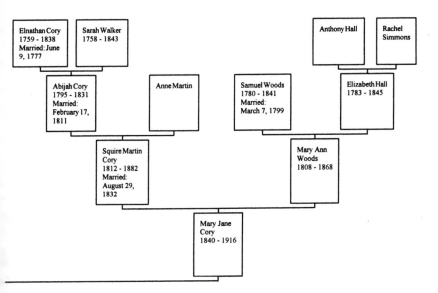

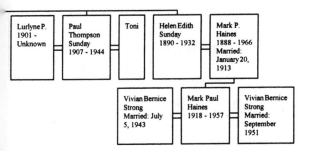

Ancestors of William Ashley Sunday

William Ashley Sunday, born November 19, 1862, in Story County IA; died November 6, 1935, in Chicago. William Ashley Sunday was buried November 9, 1935, Forest Home Cemetery, Chicago. He was the son of William A. Sunday and Mary Jane Cory. He married Helen Amelia Thompson September 5, 1888, in Chicago. She was born June 25, 1868, in Dundee IL and died February 20, 1957, in Phoenix AZ. She was the daughter of William J. Thompson and Ellen Binnie.

PARENTS

William A. Sunday, born 1828 in Chambersburg PA or Perry County PA; died December 22, 1862, in Camp Patterson MO. He was believed to be buried in an unmarked grave at Camp Patterson, but his remains were never recovered. He was the son of John Sunday and Jane. He married Mary Jane Cory October 18, 1857, in Story County IA.

Mary Jane Cory, born July 25, 1840, in Syracuse IN; died June 25, 1916, in Winona Lake IN. She was buried at Cory Burying Ground, Story County IA. She was the daughter of Squire Martin Cory and Mary Ann Woods.

Children of William A. Sunday and Mary Jane Cory*:

A. Albert Monroe Sunday, born August 3, 1858, in Story County IA; died December 12, 1900, in Nevada IA. Notes for Albert Monroe Sunday: The death date of December 12, 1900, comes from Albert's tombstone at the Cory Burying Ground, Story County IA. The Iowa Cemetery Records record Albert's death as 1893.

B. Howard Edward Sunday, born 1861 in Story County IA; died 1938 in Hood River OR; married Ellen McDonald 1882; born 1860 in Iowa; died 1937 in Hood River OR.

C. William Ashley Sunday, born November 19, 1862, in Story County IA; died November 6, 1935, in Chicago; married Helen Amelia Thompson September 5, 1888, in Chicago.

*Mary Jane Cory had two children with James M. Heizer, who would have been Billy Sunday's half-siblings. Leroy C. Heizer, born 1866 in Story County IA, died June 16, 1944 in Hood River OR, and Mary Elizabeth Heizer, born 1868 in Story County IA, died 1871 in Story County IA. Mary Jane Cory also had one child with George Stowell, a boy (name unknown) born 1876 in Boone IA, died "as a child" probably in western Kansas.

PATERNAL GRANDPARENTS

John Sunday, born 1794 in Germany; died July 1, 1849, in Mercer County OH. He was the son of Heinrich Sundag and Maryan. He married Jane.

Jane, born about 1788; died March 17, 1848, in Mercer County OH. She was
buried at Old Town Cemetery, Mercer County OH.

Children of John Sunday and Jane:

A. Barnett Sunday, born circa 1817 in Washington County PA; died circa 1850
probably in Wisconsin; married Margaret Pratt November 13, 1842; born
1821 in Washington County PA; died September 27, 1901, in Green
County WI.

B. Jeremiah Sunday, born circa 1818 in Pennsylvania; died March 6, 1855;
married (1) Harriet A. circa 1849–1850; born July 1, 1831, in Ohio; died May
23, 1852, in Mercer County OH; married (2) Jane Geller September 15, 1853.

C. Mary Ann Sunday, born August 2, 1819, in Pennsylvania; died March 9,
1880; married Amos Simmons November 22, 1845; born January 24, 1820,
in Licking County OH; died May 9, 1874, in Montevallo MO.

D. John Sunday, born 1822 in Pennsylvania; died February 23, 1899, in Mercer
County OH (county infirmary); married (1) Sarah Conner; married (2)
Catherine Stephenson 1847; born circa 1828 in Ohio; died between 1850
and 1859.

E. William A. Sunday, born 1828 in Chambersburg PA or Perry County PA;
died December 22, 1862, in Camp Patterson MO; married Mary Jane Cory
October 18, 1857, in Story County IA.

MATERNAL GRANDPARENTS

Squire Martin Cory, born June 20, 1812, in Kentucky; died October 8, 1882, in
Story County IA. He was buried at Cory Burying Ground, Story County IA.
He was the son of Abijah Cory and Anne Martin. He married (1) Mary Ann
Woods August 29, 1832, in Pickaway County OH; married (2) Charlotte A.

Mary Ann Woods, born February 17, 1808, in Ross County OH; died November
30, 1868, in Story County IA. She was buried at Cory Burying Ground,
Story County IA. She was the daughter of Samuel Woods and Elizabeth
Hall.

Children of Squire Martin Cory and Mary Ann Woods:

A. Martha M. Cory, born August 18, 1836; died May 8, 1858, in Story County IA;
married A. Brown. She was buried at Cory Burying Ground, Story County
IA.

B. Harvey Cory, born February 25, 1839; died May 26, 1860, in Story County
IA. He was buried at Cory Burying Ground, Story County IA.

C. Mary Jane Cory, born July 25, 1840, in Syracuse IN; died June 25, 1916, in
Winona Lake IN; married (1) William A. Sunday October 18, 1857, in Story

County IA; married (2) James M. Heizer August 11, 1864, in Story County IA; married (3) George Stowell September 1875 in Boone IA.

D. Miranda Cory, born May 21, 1844; died May 14, 1855, in Story County IA. She was buried at Cory Burying Ground, Story County IA.

GREAT-GRANDPARENTS (SUNDAY SURNAME)

Heinrich Sundag, born in Germany. He married Maryan. Notes for Heinrich Sundag: Also named Henry and likely changed the last name from Sundag to Sunday.

Maryan, no other information.

Children of Heinrich Sundag and Maryan:

A. John Sunday, born 1794 in Germany; died July 1, 1849, in Mercer County OH; married Jane.

B. Jacob Sunday.

C. Henry Sunday Jr.

D. Magdelena Sunday, married Rode.

E. Maryan Sunday, married Bensil.

F. Elisabeth Sunday, married Kell.

G. Christana Sunday, married Trostel.

GREAT-GRANDPARENTS (CORY SURNAME)

Abijah Cory, born 1795 in Westmoreland PA; died 1831 in Kosciusko County IN. He was the son of Elnathan Cory and Sarah Walker. He married Anne Martin February 17, 1811, in Pickaway County OH.

Anne Martin, no other information.

Children of Abijah Cory and Anne Martin:

A. Squire Martin Cory, born June 20, 1812, in Kentucky; died October 8, 1882, in Story County IA; married (1) Mary Ann Woods August 29, 1832, in Pickaway County OH; married (2) Charlotte A.

B. Isaac Cory, born 1829 in Ohio.

GREAT-GRANDPARENTS (WOODS SURNAME)

Samuel Woods, born August 12, 1780, in Northern Ireland; died September 13, 1841, in Elkhart County IN. He married Elizabeth Hall March 7, 1799, in Berkley County VA. Notes for Samuel Woods: Had a brother, William Woods.

Elizabeth Hall, born November 19, 1783, in Virginia; died March 27, 1845, in
  Elkhart County IN. She was the daughter of Anthony Hall and Rachel
  Simmons.

Children of Samuel Woods and Elizabeth Hall:

A. Martha Woods, born October 5, 1801, in Berkley County VA; died June 15,
  1830; married John Emmons January 13, 1821, in Pickaway County OH.

B. Rachel Woods, born February 12, 1803, in Berkley County VA; died 1846 in
  Elkhart County IN; married Abraham Ritchart January 10, 1823, in Pickaway
  County OH.

C. James Alexander Woods, born February 2, 1806, in Ross County OH; died
  March 22, 1886, in Polk County IA; married Anna Ritchart September 13,
  1828, in Ross County OH.

D. Mary Ann Woods, born February 17, 1808, in Ross County OH; died
  November 30, 1868, in Story County IA; married Squire Martin Cory
  August 29, 1832, in Pickaway County OH.

E. Samuel Woods Jr., born December 1, 1812, in Ohio; died October 3, 1848, in
  Elkhart County IN; married Mary Snyder.

F. John Woods, born September 15, 1813; died January 29, 1849, in Syracuse
  IN; married Mariah Moore October 25, 1837.

G. Andrew Woods, born February 13, 1816; married Sarah S. September 14,
  1841, in Kosciusko County IN.

H. Joseph Hall Woods, born October 28, 1819; died January 12, 1857, in
  Syracuse IN; married Mary Ann.

I. Miranda Woods, born January 26, 1821; married William Damon February
  29, 1844, in Elkhart County IN.

J. Benjamin Ritchart Woods, born May 4, 1824.

GREAT-GREAT-GRANDPARENTS (CORY SURNAME)

Elnathan Cory born July 9, 1759, in Elizabethtown NJ; died February 14, 1838,
  in Beaver County PA. He married Sarah Walker June 9, 1777, in
  Elizabethtown NJ. Notes for Elnathan Cory: Revolutionary War veteran.
  Served as a private in the New Jersey Militia. Had a brother, Samuel Cory.
Sarah Walker, born 1758 in New Jersey; died October 20, 1843, in Beaver
  County PA.

Children of Elnathan Cory and Sarah Walker:

A. John Cory, born January 9, 1778, in Elizabethtown NJ.

B. Ebeneezer Cory, born 1780 in Essex County NJ.

C. Levi Cory, born October 1783 in Essex County NJ.

D. Margaret Cory, born 1785 in Essex County NJ.

E. Elnathan Cory Jr. born 1788 in Westmoreland PA.

F. Mary Cory, born circa 1791.

G. Jeremiah William Cory, born September 9, 1792, in Westmoreland PA.

H. Abijah Cory, born 1795 in Westmoreland PA; died 1831 in Kosciusko County IN.

I. David Cory, born circa 1800 in Westmoreland PA.

J. Matilda Cory, born 1805 in Enon Valley, Beaver County PA.

GREAT-GREAT-GRANDPARENTS (HALL SURNAME)

Anthony Hall, no other information. He married Rachel Simmons.

Rachel Simmons, no other information.

Child of Anthony Hall and Rachel Simmons:

A. Elizabeth Hall, born November 19, 1783, in Virginia; died March 27, 1845, in Elkhart County IN. She married Samuel Woods March 7, 1799, in Berkley County VA.

Ancestors of Helen Amelia Thompson (Sunday)

Helen Amelia Thompson, born June 25, 1868, in Dundee IL; died February 20, 1957, in Phoenix AZ. She was buried February 25, 1957, at Forest Home Cemetery, Chicago. She was the daughter of William J. Thompson and Ellen Binnie. She married William Ashley Sunday September 5, 1888, in Chicago. He was born November 19, 1862, in Story County IA and died November 6, 1935, in Chicago. He was the son of William A. Sunday and Mary Jane Cory.

PARENTS

William J. Thompson, born August 1840 in Scotland; died May 1, 1909, in Chicago. He was buried May 4, 1909, at Forest Home Cemetery, Chicago. He married Ellen Binnie. Notes for William J. Thompson: Had a brother, James Thompson, born May 1835 in Scotland; died November 28, 1901, in Chicago. James Thompson was buried November 30, 1901, at Forest Home Cemetery, Chicago. He married Louise; born June 1863; died August 2, 1905, in Chicago. Louise Thompson was buried August 5, 1905, at Forest Home Cemetery, Chicago. William J. Thompson and brother, James Thompson, founded and operated Thompson Dairy in Chicago for many years.

Ellen Binnie, born July 1844 in Glascow, Scotland; died August 7, 1898, in Chicago. She was buried August 9, 1898, at Forest Home Cemetery, Chicago. She was the daughter of David Binnie and Christina Clyde.

Children of William J. Thompson and Ellen Binnie:

A. Flora Christine Thompson, born 1866 in Dundee IL; married Hopkins.
Notes for Flora Christine Thompson: Lived in Madison WI in 1935 at time
of Billy Sunday's death.

B. Helen Amelia Thompson, born June 25, 1868, in Dundee IL; died February
20, 1957, in Phoenix AZ; married William Ashley Sunday September 5,
1888, in Chicago.

C. Jennie Thompson, born 1872 in Chicago; married Campbell.

D. Ada Thompson, born 1874 in Chicago; died September 6, 1951, in Chicago.
She was buried September 10, 1951, at Forest Home Cemetery, Chicago.
She married George Spoor; born 1874 in Chicago; died November 24, 1953,
in Chicago. He was buried November 27, 1953, at Forest Home Cemetery,
Chicago.

E. William F. Thompson Jr., born September 1879 in Chicago. Notes for
William F. Thompson Jr.: Lived in Chicago in 1935 at time of Billy Sunday's
death, and his home was the place of Billy Sunday's death.

MATERNAL GRANDPARENTS

David Binnie, born in Scotland. He married Christina Clyde. Notes for David
Binnie: Came to U.S. in 1849 aboard the ship *Kahtadi* (sp?).

Christina Clyde, born in Scotland.

Children of David Binnie and Christina Clyde:

A. Ellen Binnie, born July 1844 in Glasgow, Scotland; died August 7, 1898, in
Chicago; married William J. Thompson.

B. David Binnie, born 1848 in Scotland; married Emma; born 1858 in Illinois.

Descendants of William Ashley Sunday and Helen Amelia (Thompson) Sunday

A. Helen Edith Sunday, born January 29, 1890, in Chicago; died October 12, 1932, in Sturgis MI; She was buried at Oaklawn Cemetery, Sturgis MI. She married Mark P. Haines January 20, 1913, in Winona Lake IN. He was born March 20, 1888, in Edgerton OH, and died March 3, 1966, in La Jolla CA. He was buried at Oaklawn Cemetery, Sturgis MI. Helen Edith Sunday and Mark P. Haines had one child.

B. George Marquis Sunday, born November 12, 1892, in Chicago; died September 11, 1933, in San Francisco. Notes on George Marquis Sunday: There are conflicting accounts about whether George died in Los Angeles or San Francisco. A 1933 article in Chicago revival sources file at the Morgan Library is the most thorough source, and it indicates San Francisco. His remains were buried in 1936 (three years after his death) at Forest Home Cemetery, Chicago. He married (1) Harriet Corinne Mason in 1912. She was born November 1, 1892, in Iowa, and died July 4, 1960, in San Bernadino CA. She was buried at Hollywood Forever Cemetery, Hollywood CA. George Marquis Sunday married (2) Mauryne (Renee) Reichard June 1931 in San Francisco. George Marquis Sunday and Harriet Corinne Mason had two children. Notes for Harriet Corinne Mason: Harriet Mason Sunday took on the responsibility for rearing her grandson, Marquis Ashley Sunday, shortly after he was born. She remained his primary care giver throughout his formative years.

C. William Ashley Sunday Jr., born June 15, 1901, in Chicago; died April 2, 1938, in Los Angeles. Notes on William Ashley Sunday Jr.: There is a death date discrepancy between April 2, 3, and 4, 1938, from different sources. He was buried April 6, 1938, at Forest Home Cemetery, Chicago. He married (1) Millicent. He married (2) Mae Sanders 1926 in Tijuana, Mexico. He again married (3) Mae Sanders May 5, 1928, in Yuma AZ. He married (4) Nina October 19, 1929, in Mexicali, Mexico. William Ashley Sunday Jr. had no children.

D. Paul Thompson Sunday, born June 15, 1907, in Chicago; died February 24, 1944, in Palmdale CA. He was buried March 13, 1944, at Forest Home Cemetery, Chicago. He married (1) Lurlyne P.; born 1901 in Arkansas. He married (2) Toni. Paul Thompson Sunday had no children.

Child of Helen Edith Sunday and Mark P. Haines:

A. Mark Paul Haines, born April 11, 1918, in Sturgis MI; died May 13, 1957, in Phoenix AZ. He was buried at Oaklawn Cemetery, Sturgis MI. He married (1) Vivian Bernice Strong July 5, 1943; born in Klamath Falls OR. He again married (2) Vivian Bernice Strong September 1951 in Arizona. Mark Paul Haines had no children.

Children of George Marquis Sunday and Harriet Corinne Mason:

A. George Marquis Sunday Jr., born March 27, 1914, in Washington; died 1968. Notes on George Marquis Sunday Jr.: A letter (Morgan Library Collection) from George M. Sunday Jr. to Helen A. Sunday dated March 27, 1952, which mentions that he turned thirty-eight years of age that day, is the only documentation of this data. He married (1) Alma Baine in 1940. She was born April 1, 1918, and died January 30, 1997, at the U.S. consulate, in Vienna, Austria. He married (2) Cynthia. He married (3) Lillian. Lillian died December 1976 in Wheaton IL. George Marquis Sunday Jr. and Alma Baine had one child.

B. John M. Sunday, born May 1916 in Pennsylvania; died July 25, 1934 in Los Angeles. He was buried at Hollywood Forever Cemetery, Hollywood CA. John M. Sunday had no children.

GREAT-GRANDCHILDREN

Child of George Marquis Sunday Jr. and Alma Baine:

A. Marquis Ashley Sunday, born August 15, 1940, in Los Angeles; died March 22, 1982, in San Francisco. Notes for Marquis Ashley Sunday: He was killed in a homicide in San Francisco, March 22, 1982, San Francisco Police Department case # 82-1332329, San Francisco Medical Examiner's report # 1982-0439. Assailant was Barbara Barnato, with whom Marquis was living. His remains were handled by Mission Chapels Funeral Home in San Francisco. No claim was made of his personal property. The $25.50 on his person at the time of his death was turned over to the San Francisco City Treasurer's Office, and his personal property, including a watch, wallet, pocketknife, and ring, were sold at public auction for $10.00. Marquis Ashley Sunday is not believed to have had any children.

Notes

1. Homespun and Cashmere

1. James Deetz, *In Small Things Forgotten*, pp. 17–18.

2. Lyle Dorsett, *Billy Sunday and the Redemption of Urban America*, p. 7.

3. Ibid., p. 8.

4. Robert F. Martin, *Hero of the Heartland*, p. 5.

5. Ibid., pp. 19–21.

6. Dorsett, *Billy Sunday*, p. 11.

7. Lee Thomas, *The Billy Sunday Story*, pp. 54–58.

8. Helen A. Sunday, *Ma Sunday Still Speaks*, p. 23.

9. Ibid., pp. 20–21.

10. William A. Sunday, *Autobiography of Billy Sunday*, p. 7.

11. Sunday, *Ma Sunday Still Speaks*, p. 5.

12. Theodore Thomas Frankenberg, *Billy Sunday*, p. 62.

13. Sunday, *Autobiography*, p. 49.

2. Caught on the Fly

1. James Deetz, *Invitation to Archaeology*, pp. 83–96.

2. Roger Bruns, *Preacher*, p. 29.

3. Betty Steele Everett, *Sawdust Trail Preacher*, pp. 11–12.

4. Dorsett, *Billy Sunday*, p. 18.

5. William G. McLoughlin Jr., *Billy Sunday Was His Real Name*, p. 5.

6. Bruns, *Preacher*, p. 48.

7. Sunday, *Ma Sunday Still Speaks*, p. 14.

8. Ibid., p. 7.

9. Wendy Knickerbocker, *Sunday at the Ballpark*, pp. 81–83.

10. Frankenberg, *Billy Sunday*, p. 62.

11. Dorsett, *Billy Sunday*, p. 28.

12. Elijah Brown, *The Real Billy Sunday*, pp. 36–37.

13. Ibid., p. 112.

14. Knickerbocker, *Sunday at the Ballpark*, p. 83.

15. Dorsett, *Billy Sunday*, p. 115.

16. Sunday, *Ma Sunday Still Speaks*, p. 43.

17. Dorsett, *Billy Sunday*, p. 41.

18. Robert A. Allen, *Billy Sunday*, p. 65.

3. Revival Machine

1. Melton Wright, *Giant for God*, p. 27.

2. Bruns, *Preacher*, p. 88.

3. Sunday, *Ma Sunday Still Speaks*, p. 9.

4. Thomas, *The Billy Sunday Story*, p. 73.

5. John King, interview.

6. George M. Marsden, *Fundamentalism and American Culture*, pp. 3–5, 91–93.

7. "Rev. Billy Sunday's Sermons, Prayers and Epigrams," p. 58.

8. *Charlotte Observer*, February 10, 1924.

9. Thomas, *The Billy Sunday Story*, pp. 183–184.

10. William Lloyd Clark, ed., *Billy Sunday U-N-M-A-S-K-E-D*, pp. 17–18.

11. Thomas, *The Billy Sunday Story*, p. 69.

12. McLoughlin, *Billy Sunday Was His Real Name*, p. 165.

13. Ibid., p. 278.

14. D. Bruce Lockerbie, *Billy Sunday*, p. 43.

15. Mary Margaret Cawthon, "A Descriptive Analysis of the Homiletical Career of William A. (Billy) Sunday," pp. 41–44.

16. Felix Cox, "Billy Sunday, Evangelist and Entertainer," pp. 8–12.

17. Brown, *The Real Billy Sunday*, pp. 137–148.

18. Homer Rodeheaver, *Twenty Years with Billy Sunday*, p. 20.

19. Sunday, *Ma Sunday Still Speaks*, pp. 25–28.

20. Rodeheaver, *Twenty Years with Billy Sunday*, p. 94.

21. Dorsett, *Billy Sunday*, p. 98.

22. Larry G. Anderson, personal communication.

23. Theodore Dreiser, *A Hoosier Holiday*, pp. 29–30.

24. Sinclair Lewis, *Elmer Gantry*, p. 7.

25. Dorsett, *Billy Sunday*, p. 93.

26. Cawthon, "A Descriptive Analysis," p. 64.

27. Cox, "Billy Sunday," pp. 14–15.

28. Lindsay Denison, "The Rev. Billy Sunday and His War on the Devil," pp. 464–467.

29. Gerald William Bieber, "Billy Sunday," p. 25.

30. Sunday, *Ma Sunday Still Speaks*, p. 39.

31. Thomas, *The Billy Sunday Story*, p. 91.

32. Robert Edward Davis, "Billy Sunday," p. 95.

33. Dorsett, *Billy Sunday*, p. 117.

34. Homer Rodeheaver, ed., *More Worthwhile Poems*; Bert Wilhoit, *Rody*, pp. 25–26.

35. Dorsett, *Billy Sunday*, pp. 134–138.

4. For the Love of a Nation

1. Martin Marty, *Pilgrims in Their Own Land*, pp. 352–353.

2. Irvin G. Wylie, "The Socialist Press and the Libel Laws," p. 76.

3. Sunday Papers, Sermon Notes, Reel 15.

4. Ibid., Reel 10.

5. Dorsett, *Billy Sunday*, p. 105.

6. Thomas, *The Billy Sunday Story*, p. 185.

7. Ibid., p. 114.

8. Bruns, *Preacher*, p. 206.

9. Ibid., p. 210.

10. Ibid., pp. 257–258.

11. Sunday, *Ma Sunday Still Speaks*, p. 24.

12. Dorsett, *Billy Sunday*, p. 49.

13. Bruns, *Preacher*, p. 142.

14. Brown, *The Real Billy Sunday*, pp. 150–152.

15. Lockerbie, *Billy Sunday*, pp. 25–31.

16. Ibid., pp. 28–31.

17. William A. Sunday, *Get on the Water Wagon*, p. 1.

18. Emmett Gowen, "Still Raid," reprinted in Wright, *Giant for God*, pp. 95–104.

19. George Mills, *Rogues and Heroes from Iowa's Amazing Past*, p. 122.

20. Larry Engelmann, "Billy Sunday," pp. 20–21.

21. Bruns, *Preacher*, pp. 172–175.

22. Frankenberg, *Billy Sunday*, p. 175.

23. John Fea, "The Town that Billy Sunday Could Not Shut Down," pp. 256–257.

24. Albert Peterson, *Highlights along the Sawdust Trail*, p. 9.

25. Bruns, *Preacher*, p. 174.

26. Lewis, *Elmer Gantry*, p. 262.

5. At Home in Winona Lake

1. Thomas, *The Billy Sunday Story*, pp. 118, 123.

2. Charles Dickens, *A Christmas Carol*, pp. 56–57.

3. Gillian Naylor, *The Arts and Crafts Movement*, p. 13.

4. Adrian Tinniswood, *The Arts and Crafts House*, p. 12.

5. Ibid., p. 6.

6. Linda Parry, ed. *William Morris*, pp. 274–275.

7. *Arts and Crafts Essays by Members of the Arts and Crafts Exhibition Society*, p. 34.

8. Gustav Stickley, *Craftsman Homes*, pp. 196–197.

9. Sunday, *Ma Sunday Still Speaks*, pp. 14, 48.

10. Ibid., p. 55.

11. Ibid., p. 16.

12. Stickley, *Craftsman Homes*, p. 187.

13. Tod M. Volpe and Beth Cathers, *Treasures of the American Arts and Crafts Movement 1890–1920*, p. 168.

14. Theodore Thomas Frankenberg, *The Spectacular Career of Rev. Billy Sunday*, p. 192.

15. Ibid.

16. Sunday, *Ma Sunday Still Speaks*, pp. 20–23.

17. Thomas, *The Billy Sunday Story*, p. 125.

18. Lee Thomas, *Billy I*, p. 112.

Epilogue

1. Jane Powell Fesler, interview.

2. Frankenberg, *The Spectacular Career of Rev. Billy Sunday*, p. 158.

3. Carl Sandburg, *Billy Sunday and Other Poems*, p. 4.

4. Sunday, *Autobiography*, p. 50.

Bibliography

Address by Billy Sunday. Philadelphia: Law Enforcement League of Philadelphia, 1922.

Alexandria Times Tribune. Alexandria, Indiana, 1931.

Allen, Robert A. *Billy Sunday: Home Run to Heaven*. Milford, Michigan: Mott Media, 1985.

American Legion Sunday Evening Club Program, LaGrange, Illinois, 1935.

Anderson Daily Bulletin. Anderson, Indiana, 1931.

Anderson, Larry G. Personal communication with author. Greencastle, Indiana, 2004.

Arts and Crafts Essays by Members of the Arts and Crafts Exhibition Society. London: Longmans Green and Company, 1893.

Atchison, G. A. *Billy Sunday in Kansas City: The Story of a Great Campaign Day by Day*. Trenton, New Jersey: Self-published, 1916.

Atlanta Constitution. Atlanta, 1917.

Atlantic News. Atlantic, Iowa, 1902.

Audubon County Journal. Exira, Iowa, 1901.

Austin Herald. Austin, Minnesota, 1906.

Bangor Daily News. Bangor, Maine, 1927.

Bentley, Craig A. Personal communication with author. Columbus Revival Heritage Museum and Society, Columbus, Ohio, 2004–2005.

Betts, Frederick W. *Billy Sunday: The Man and Method*. Boston: Murray Press, 1916.

Bieber, Gerald William. "Billy Sunday: A Study of His Message during the Second Decade of the Twentieth Century, and the Means He Used to Persuade His Audiences." Ph.D. diss., University of Minnesota, 1968.

Billy Sunday Boston Revival Souvenir. Boston: Up to Date Publishing Company, 1916.

Billy Sunday Revival Campaign Project. Morgan Library Collection, Grace College, Winona Lake, Indiana, 1995.

Billy Sunday Speaks! One Thousand Epigrams of the World-Famous Evangelist. Grand Rapids, Michigan: Zondervan Publishing House, 1937.

Billy Sunday's Sermons. Detroit: Detroit Times, 1916.

Bristol Herald-Courier. Bristol, Tennessee-Virginia, 1920.

Brooklyn Eagle. Brooklyn, New York, 1890 and 1902.

Brown, Elijah. *The Real Billy Sunday*. New York: Fleming H. Revell Company, 1914.

Bruns, Roger A. *Preacher: Billy Sunday and Big-Time American Evangelism*. New York: W. W. Norton and Company, 1992.

Bureau County Republican. Princeton, Illinois, 1906.

Burlington Hawk-eye. Burlington, Iowa, 1905.

Calkins, David L. "Billy Sunday's Cincinnati Crusade." *Cincinnati Historical Society Bulletin* 27, no. 4 (1969): 292–302.

Canon City Record. Canon City, Colorado, 1905.

Canton Repository. Canton, Ohio, 1911–1912.

Cawthon, Mary Margaret. "A Descriptive Analysis of the Homiletical Career of

William A. (Billy) Sunday." M.A. thesis, Auburn University, 1965.

Cedar Rapids Gazette. Cedar Rapids, Iowa, 1909.

Charlotte Observer. Charlotte, North Carolina, 1923–1924.

Chatterbox: Danville High School Weekly Paper. Danville, Virginia, 1922.

Clark, William Lloyd, ed. *Billy Sunday U-N-M-A-S-K-E-D*. Milan, Illinois: Rail Splitter Press, 1929.

Clarksville Star. Clarksville, Iowa, 1898.

Cleveland Daily Banner. Cleveland, Tennessee, 1935.

Cleveland Plain Dealer. Cleveland, Ohio, 1935.

Columbia Record. Columbia, South Carolina, 1923.

Columbus Citizen. Columbus, Ohio, 1912–1913.

Columbus Dispatch. Columbus, Ohio, 1912–1913.

Corydon Democrat. Corydon, Iowa, 1901.

Cox, Felix. "Billy Sunday, Evangelist and Entertainer: The Use of Consumer Culture in Evangelism." M.M. degree project, Yale Institute of Sacred Music, 1994.

Crandall, William S. and Roy D. Lewis. *History of Boulevard Methodist Church, 1907–1954*. Binghamton, New York: Boulevard Methodist Church, 1954.

Daily Free Press. Carbondale, Illinois, 1907.

Daily Republican. Belvidere, Illinois, 1902.

Davis, Robert Edward. "Billy Sunday: Preacher-Showman." *Southern Speech Journal* 32, no. 2 (1966): 83–97.

Decatur Herald. Decatur, Illinois, 1908.

Deetz, James. *In Small Things Forgotten: The Archaeology of Early American Life*. New York: Doubleday, 1977.

———. *Invitation to Archaeology*. Garden City, New York: Natural History Press, 1967.

Denison, Lindsay. "The Rev. Billy Sunday and His War on the Devil." *American Magazine* 64, no. 5 (1907): 450–468.

Denver Post. Denver, 1914, 1918, 1927, 1929, 1931.

Des Moines Tribune. Des Moines, Iowa, 1914, 1921, 1926.

Detroit News. Detroit, 1927, 1928, 1930, 1932, 1934.

Dickens, Charles. *A Christmas Carol*. London: Bradbury and Evans, 1843; reprinted in *A Christmas Carol—The Editha Series*. New York and Boston: H. M. Caldwell Company, 1902.

Dorsett, Lyle. *Billy Sunday and the Redemption of Urban America*. Grand Rapids, Michigan: William B. Erdmans Publishing Company, 1991.

Dreiser, Theodore. *A Hoosier Holiday*. 1916. Reprint, Bloomington: Indiana University Press, 1997.

Duluth Evening Herald. Duluth, Minnesota, 1918.

Durham, N. W. *History of the City of Spokane and Spokane County Washington*. Spokane, Washington: S. J. Clarke Publishing Company, 1912.

East Liverpool Morning Tribune. East Liverpool, Ohio, 1912.

Ellis, William T. *Billy Sunday: The Man and His Message*. Swarthmore, Pennsylvania: L.T. Myers, 1914.

Elyria Chronicle Telegram. Elyria, Ohio, 1929.

Engelmann, Larry D. "Billy Sunday: 'God, You've Got a Job on Your Hands in Detroit.'" *Michigan History Magazine* 55, no. 1 (1971): 1–21.

Erie Herald. Erie, Pennsylvania, 1911.

Everett, Betty Steele. *Sawdust Trail Preacher: The Story of Billy Sunday*. Fort Washington, Pennsylvania: Christian Literature Crusade, 1987.

Fairmount News. Fairmount, Indiana, 1902.

Fargo Forum. Fargo, North Dakota, 1912.

Fea, John. "The Town That Billy Sunday Could Not Shut Down: Prohibition and Sunday's Chicago Crusade of 1918." *Illinois Historical Journal* 87, no. 4 (1994): 242–258.

Fesler, Jane Powell. Interview by William A. Firstenberger. Billy Sunday Historic Site Museum, South Bend, Indiana, 2000.

Fike, Nancy. Personal communication with author. McHenry County Historical Society, McHenry, Illinois, 2004.

First Annual Program—Rockville Chautauqua. Rockville, Indiana: Rockville Chautauqua Association, 1911.

Firstenberger, William A. "Materials of an Anti-Materialist: An Interpretation of the Baseball Evangelist, Billy Sunday, through an Examination of Material Culture at His Home in Winona Lake, Indiana." M.L.S. thesis, Indiana University South Bend, 2000.

Florida Times-Union. Jacksonville, Florida, 1920.

Frankenberg, Theodore Thomas. *Billy Sunday: His Tabernacles and Sawdust Trails.* Columbus, Ohio: F. J. Heer Printing Company Publishers, 1917.

———. *The Spectacular Career of Rev. Billy Sunday.* Columbus, Ohio: McClelland & Company, 1913.

Gaerte, Douglas M. "Justifying Social and Political Involvement: A Case Study in the Rhetoric of Billy Sunday." M.A. thesis, Indiana University, 1987.

Galesburg Mail. Galesburg, Illinois, 1907.

Galva Weekly News. Galva, Illinois, 1904.

Georgian. Atlanta, 1917.

Gowen, Emmett. "Still Raid: Featuring Billy Sunday." *Scribner's Magazine,* 1935, reprinted in Melton Wright, *Giant for God.*

Greensboro Daily News. Greensboro, North Carolina, 1925.

Gullen, Karyn, ed. *Billy Sunday Speaks.* New York: Chelsea House Publishers, 1981.

Hall, Joseph H. "Sunday in St. Louis: The Anatomy and Anomaly of a Large-Scale Billy Sunday Revival in St. Louis." Covenant Theological Seminary, 1984.

Hancock Signal. Garner, Iowa, 1896.

Harlan Tribune. Harlan, Iowa, 1901.

Heritage of Vermillion County. Danville, Illinois: Vermillion County Illinois Museum Society, 1982.

History of Hancock County, Illinois. Carthage, Illinois: Board of Supervisors of Hancock County, 1968.

"Images of the Past in the City of Roses." *Southeast Missourian,* 1993.

Iowa County Advertiser. Parnell, Iowa, 1898.

Jacksonville Journal. Jacksonville, Illinois, 1908.

Jefferson Bee. Jefferson, Iowa, 1904.

Jenson, Richard K. *The Billy Pulpits.* Collierville, Tennessee: First Foundations, 1996.

King, John. Interview by Robert Cook for *Across Indiana.* WFYI, Indianapolis, 1998.

Knickerbocker, Wendy. *Sunday at the Ballpark: Billy Sunday's Professional Baseball Career, 1883–1890.* Lanham, Maryland: Scarecrow Press, 2000.

Knoxville Sentinel. Knoxville, Tennessee, 1923.

Lakeside News. Lakeside, Ohio, 1932.

Lamb, George. *Every Day Was Sunday When Billy Came to Town.* Dixon, Illinois: P&M Enterprises, 1971.

Lancaster Camp Grounds Hotel Register.

Stanton Prior, Lancaster Camp Grounds Historical Society, Lancaster, Ohio, 2005.

Leonard, Doris. *Big Bureau and Bright Prairies: A History of Bureau County.* Princeton, Illinois: Bureau County Board of Supervisors, 1968.

Lewis, Sinclair. *Elmer Gantry.* New York: Harcourt, Brace, and Company, 1927.

Lockerbie, D. Bruce. *Billy Sunday.* Waco, Texas: Word Books, 1965.

"Looking Back." *The Repository* (Canton, Ohio), 1981.

Los Angeles Times. Los Angeles, 1917.

Marsden, George M. *Fundamentalism and American Culture: The Shaping of Twentieth-Century Evangelicalism, 1870–1925.* New York: Oxford University Press, 1980.

Martin, Robert F. *Hero of the Heartland: Billy Sunday and the Transformation of American Society, 1862–1935.* Bloomington: Indiana University Press, 2002.

Marty, Martin. *Pilgrims in Their Own Land: 500 Years of Religion in America.* New York: Penguin Books, 1984.

Mason City Globe-Gazette. Mason City, Iowa, 1905.

McLoughlin, William G., Jr. *Billy Sunday Was His Real Name.* Chicago: University of Chicago Press, 1955.

Memphis Press Scimitar. Memphis, Tennessee, 1935.

Miksell, Charlotte. Interview by William Firstenberger and Brent Wilcoxson, Billy Sunday Historic Site Museum, Winona Lake, Indiana, 1998.

Mills, George. *Rogues and Heroes from Iowa's Amazing Past.* Ames: Iowa State University Press, 1972.

Monmouth Daily Review Atlas. Monmouth, Illinois, 1926.

Muscatine Journal. Muscatine, Iowa, 1907.

Naylor, Gillian. *The Arts and Crafts Movement.* Cambridge: Massachusetts Institute of Technology Press, 1971.

New Castle Herald. New Castle, Pennsylvania, 1910.

News-Democrat. Carrollton, Kentucky, 2004.

News-Herald. Franklin, Pennsylvania, 1931.

Nuet, D. James. Personal communication with author. Elkhart, Indiana, 2002.

Ohio State Journal. Columbus, Ohio, 1923, 1935.

Omaha Daily News. Omaha, Nebraska, 1916.

Orton, Trevor, ed. *"Billy" Sunday Spokane Campaign: December–January–February 1908–1909.* Souvenir booklet. Spokane, Washington: Western Colportage Association, 1909.

Ottumwa Courier. Ottumwa, Iowa, 1908.

Parker, Mac. *Billy Sunday Meetings.* Tampa, Florida: Tribune Press, 1919.

Parry, Linda, ed. *William Morris.* London: Philip Wilson Publishers, 1996.

Paynesville Press. Paynesville, Minneosta, 1931.

Pendleton Tribune. Pendleton, Oregon, 1919.

Peterson, Albert. *Highlights along the Sawdust Trail.* Chillicothe, Iowa: Self-published, no date.

Phillips, Edward. "History of Wilkes-Barre, Luzerne County, Pennsylvania." Unpublished manuscript, no date.

Phillips, Rachael M. *Billy Sunday: Evangelist on the Sawdust Trail.* Uhrichsville, Ohio: Barbour Books, 2001.

Pittsburgh Press. Pittsburgh Pennsylvania, 1914.

Pitzer, Donald Elden. "The Ohio Campaigns of Billy Sunday with Special Emphasis upon the 1913 Columbus Revival." MA thesis, Ohio State University, Columbus, Ohio, 1962.

Pontiac Leader. Pontiac, Illinois, 1904.

Portland Press Herald. Portland, Maine, 1927.

Portsmouth Blade. Portsmouth, Ohio, 1911.

Portsmouth Star. Norfolk–Portsmouth, Virginia, 1920.

Prophetstown Echo. Prophetstown, Illinois, 1906.

Redwood Gazette. Redwood Falls, Minnesota, 1904–1905.

"Rev. Billy Sunday's Sermons, Prayers and Epigrams." *Richmond (Indiana) Item,* 1922.

"Rites Saturday for 'Ma' Sunday." *Warsaw (Indiana) Times-Union,* 1957.

Roanoke Times. Roanoke, Virginia, 1920, 1921, 1928.

Rochester Daily Bulletin. Rochester, Minnesota, 1905–1906.

Rodeheaver, Homer. *Twenty Years with Billy Sunday.* Nashville, Tennessee: Cokesbury Press, 1936.

———, ed. *More Worthwhile Poems.* Winona Lake, Indiana: Rodeheaver Hall-Mack Company, 1945.

Rose, Arthur P. *An Illustrated History of Nobles County Minnesota.* Worthington, Minnesota: Northern History Publishing Company, 1908.

Rose, William Ganson. *Cleveland: The Making of a City.* Cleveland: World Publishing Company, 1990.

St. Louis Globe Democrat. St. Louis, 1928.

Sanford, Joseph M. *Billy Sunday—His Life as Seen through Picture Postcards,* vols. 1–2, 1st ed. Willingboro, New Jersey: Self-published CD-ROM, 2004.

Sandburg, Carl. *Billy Sunday and Other Poems.* New York: Harcourt, Brace and Company, 1993.

Shand, Norman. Personal communication with author. Franklin Lakes, New Jersey, 2005.

Shick, Nancy. *Portrait and Biographical*

History of Charleston, Illinois. Charleston, Illinois: Rardin Graphics, 1985.

Shuster, Robert, ed. *A Guide to the Microfilm Edition of the Papers of William and Helen Sunday 1882–1974.* Wheaton, Illinois: The Billy Graham Center at Wheaton College, 1978.

Sigourney News. Sigourney, Iowa, 1896.

Silver City History Book. Silver City, Iowa: Auxiliary Unit to Gordon May Post 439 American Legion of Iowa, 1954.

Southern Illinois Herald. Carbondale, Illinois, 1907.

State. Columbia, South Carolina, 1923.

Sterling Daily Gazette. Sterling, Illinois, 1904, 1927, 1946.

Stickley, Gustav. *Craftsman Homes: Architecture and Furnishings of the American Arts and Crafts Movement.* New York: Craftsman Publishing Company, 1909. Reprint, New York: Dover Publications, 1979.

Stocker, Fern Neal. *Billy Sunday: Baseball Preacher.* Chicago: Moody Press, 1985.

Story County Genealogical Society, comp. *Story County, Iowa: Grave Marker Inscriptions.* Des Moines, Iowa: Iowa Genealogical Society, 1993.

Sunday, Helen A. *Ma Sunday Still Speaks.* Winona Lake, Indiana: Winona Lake Christian Assembly, 1957.

Sunday, William A. *Autobiography of Billy Sunday.* Winona Lake, Indiana: Mrs. W. A. Sunday/Winona Christian Assembly and Bible Conference, [ca. 1948].

———. *Get on the Water Wagon.* Sturgis, Michigan: Journal Publishing Company, 1914.

Thomas, Lee. *Billy I.* Van Nuys, California: Son-Rise Books–Bible Voice, 1974.

———. *The Billy Sunday Story.* Grand

Rapids, Michigan: Zondervan
Publishing House, 1961.

Tinniswood, Adrian. *The Arts and Crafts House*. New York: Watson-Guptill Publications, 1999.

Toledo Blade. Toledo, Ohio, 1911.

University Daily Kansan. Robinson, Kansas, April–May, 1916.

Volpe, Tod M., and Beth Cathers. *Treasures of the American Arts and Crafts Movement 1890–1920*. New York: Harry N. Abrams, 1988.

W. A. Sunday Meetings at Springfield, Illinois. Souvenir booklet. Springfield, Illinois: no publisher, 1909.

Wapello Republican. Wapello, Iowa, 1935.

Waterloo Reporter. Waterloo, Iowa, 1910.

Whalin, W. Terry. *Billy Sunday*. Uhrichsville, Ohio: Barbour Publishing, 1996.

Wilhoit, Bert. *Rody: Memories of Homer Rodeheaver*. Greenville, South Carolina: Bob Jones University Press, 2000.

Wilkes-Barre Record. Wilkes-Barre, Pennsylvania, 1913, 1930.

William and Helen Sunday Archives. Morgan Library, Grace College, Winona Lake, Indiana.

Williamsport Sun. Williamsport, Pennsylvania, 1913, 1925.

Winona Assembly Summer Program Yearbooks 1896–1935. Winona Lake, Ind.: Winona Christian Assembly and Summer Schools.

Winston-Salem Journal. Winston-Salem, North Carolina, 1925.

Wright, Melton. *Giant for God: A Biography of the Life of William Ashley ("Billy") Sunday*. Boyce, Virginia: Carr Publishing Company, 1951.

Wylie, Irvin G. "The Socialist Press and the Libel Laws: A Case Study." *Midwest Journal*, 4 (1952): 72–79.

Youngstown Vindicator. Youngstown, Ohio, 1908–1910.

Index

Ackley, B. D., 124
Albany, Texas, 6
Alexander, Homer, 124
Anderson, Edith. *See* Edith Anderson
  Butler
amusements, 56, 64–66, 70
Anson, Adrian "Cap," 12, 18
Anti-Saloon League, 43
Art Nouveau movement, 87
Arts and Crafts movement, 81–93, 97
Asher, Virginia, 39, 53, 124
Asher, William, 124
Aurora, Illinois, 17

Baine, Alma. *See* Alma Baine Sunday
Baltimore, Maryland, 30, 41
Barnato, Barbara, 127, 137
Barr, G. Walter, 124
baseball, 12–17, 20–21, 68, 105
Beckwith, Paul, 124
Bethany Presbyterian Church, 25
Billy Sunday Pudding, 40
Binnie, David, 135
Binnie, David, Jr., 135
Binnie, Ellen. *See* Ellen Binnie Thompson
Boston, Massachusetts, 51
Brann, William Cowper, 31–32
Brewster, George Ashley, 124
Brown, A., 131
Brown, Elijah P., 43, 49–50, 124
Bryan, William Jennings, 72, 74
Buffalo, New York, 41
Bundy, John Elwood, 41
Butler, Charles, 124
Butler, Edith Anderson, 124
Butterfield, William, 124

Campbell, Archie, 7, 10
Campbell, Mr., 135
Cardiff, John, 124

Carter, Howard, 41
Chandler, A. B., 17
Chapman, J. Wilbur, 24–26, 63, 78
Charlotte, North Carolina, 30
Chautauqua movement, 25, 36
Chicago, Illinois, 19, 51, 60, 72
Chicago White Stockings (Cubs), 12–13,
  15–17, 68
Christian Endeavor Society, 9
Cincinnati Reds, 21
Clarke, Harry, 124
Clyde, Christina, 135
Cody, William "Buffalo Bill," 43
Collison, William, 124
Conner, Sarah, 131
Connett, Mrs., 124
conversions. *See* appendix B
Coolidge, Calvin, 56
Cory, Abijah, 129, 131, 132, 133
Cory, Anne Martin, 129, 131, 132
Cory, Charlotte A., 6, 131, 132
Cory, David, 134
Cory, Ebeneezer, 133
Cory, Elnathan, 129, 132, 133
Cory, Elnathan, Jr., 134
Cory, Harvey, 131
Cory, Isaac, 132
Cory, Jeremiah William, 134
Cory, John, 133
Cory, Levi, 133
Cory, Margaret, 133
Cory, Martha M., 131
Cory, Mary, 134
Cory, Mary Ann Woods, 6, 129, 130, 131,
  132, 133
Cory, Mary Jane. *See* Mary Jane "Jennie"
  Cory Heizer Stowell Sunday
Cory, Miranda, 132
Cory, Matilda, 134
Cory, Samuel, 133

Cory, Sarah Walker, 129, 132, 133
Cory, Squire Martin, 2, 6, 130, 131, 132, 133
Creel, George, 34
Cubs baseball team. *See* Chicago White
  Stockings
Curtis, Charles, 43
Curtiss, Glenn, 33

Dale, Otis G., 124
Damon, William, 133
Darwin, Charles, 29
Debs, Eugene V., 58–59
DeMille, Cecil B., 44
Democratic Party, 59, 72
Dickens, Charles, 82
Dickey, Solomon, 78
Dowey, George G., 124
Dreiser, Theodore, 40
Dundee, Illinois, 7

Eisenhower, Dwight D., 56
Elgin, Illinois, 45
Ellis, William T., 64
Emmet, Ed, 124
Emmons, John, 133
Erie, Pennsylvania, 45
Evanston Academy, 14, 19
evolution, 29

Fairbanks, Douglas, 17
Fesler, Jane Powell, 104
Fetterolf, Rose M., 124
Finney, Charles G., 65
Fischer, Mr. and Mrs. Fred, 124
Forest Home Cemetery, 103
Franchere, Miss, 124
Frank, J. Glenn, 124
Frick, Ford, 17, 56
Freud, Sigmund, 61
Fundamentalism, 21, 26, 29, 38

Gamlin, Alice, 125
Gantry, Elmer, 40, 75
Garner, Iowa, 25–26
Geller, Jane, 131

Gibbons, James, 30
Gill, Mr. and Mrs. Albert Price, 125
Grant, Ulysses S., 59

Haines, Helen. *See* Helen Edith Sunday
Haines, Mark Paul, 100, 127, 129, 136,
  137
Haines, Vivian Bernice Strong, 129, 137
Hall, Anthony, 129, 133, 134
Hall, Elizabeth. *See* Elizabeth Hall Woods
Hall, Rachel Simmons, 129, 133, 134
Hammontree, Homer, 125
Harding, Warren G., 56
Harper, Mr. and Mrs., 125
Haymaker, Willis, 125
Heinz, H. J., 33, 43
Heizer, James M. "Matt," 2, 6, 130, 132
Heizer, Leroy C., 130
Heizer, Mary Elizabeth, 130
Honeywell, I. E., 125
Hood River, Oregon, 81
Hoover, Herbert, 56, 59
Hopkins, Mr., 135
Hughes, Charles E., 43

industrial revolution, 32, 81–83
Ingersoll, Robert G., 32, 40
Iowa Soldiers Orphan Home, 2–4, 6

Jenkins, Walter, 125
Johnson, James "Uncle Jimmy," 125
Johnson, Wade Hampton, 125
Johnston, Howard A., 125
Jones, Bob, Sr., 43
Johnson, Walter, 17
Johnson, William "Pussyfoot," 72
Jolson, Al, 106

Kinney, Florence, 125
Knoxville, Iowa, 41
Kresge, S. S., 33
Ku Klux Klan, 29–31

Lamont, Jean, 125
Landis, Kenesaw Mountain, 17

Latham, Arlie, 18
Laughlin, Hugh, 125
Leland, Henry, 33
Lewis, Sinclair, 40
Lincoln, Abraham, 59–60
Linden, John, 125
Locke, Willis, 125
Lorimer, Mamie, 125
Lynn, Nora, 45, 98–100, 102–103

MacDonald, A. B., 125
MacLaren, Anna, 125
Marshalltown, Iowa, 12
Martin, Anne. *See* Anne Martin Cory
Marx, Karl, 61
Mason, Harriet Corinne. *See* Harriet
   Corinne Mason Sunday
Matthews, Robert, 125
Mayo, C. H., 43–44
Mayo, W. A., 44
McDonald, Ellen, 130
Memphis, Tennessee, 69
Miller, Frances, 125
Mishawaka, Indiana, 104
Modernism, 29–32
Moody, Dwight L., 21, 63–64, 77
Moore, Mariah, 133
Morris, William, 82–83, 89
Moses, 59
Mount Hood: architectural style, 81–89,
   97; floor plan layout, 94, 96–100, 106;
   intact collection of, 1; location in
   Winona Lake, 78, 92; naming of, 81;
   outdoor landscape, 77–78, 92, 94–96
Muirhead, Rae, 125

Nation, Carrie, 72
Nevada, Iowa, 11–12
New York City, New York, 51–60
Nietzsche, Friedrich, 61
Northwestern University, 14–16
Nutting, Wallace, 90

Oliver, French, 125
Oliver, Joseph D., 105

Pacific Garden Mission, 18–20, 63
Peacock, L. K., 125
Perry, Iowa, 45
Pershing, John J. "Black Jack," 62
Peterson, Albert, 125
Peterson, Roy, 125
Philadelphia, Pennsylvania revival, 41, 43,
   46, 48–49
Philadelphia Phillies, 12, 16, 21
Pittsburgh Alleghenies (Pirates), 12, 15–16
Pittsburgh, Pennsylvania, 41
Pitzer, Harland H., 125
Pledger, Clifton Pryor, 126
Poxen, Miss, 126
Pratt, Margaret, 131
Presbyterians, 7, 9–10, 25
Prohibition, 24, 32, 36, 64, 68–75
Pugin, A. W. N., 82
Pullman Railcar Company, 51–53

race relations, 29–30
Rapp, Fred W., 126
Red Cross, 60
Reichard, Mauryne Renee. *See* Mauryne
   Renee Reichard Sunday
Republican Party, 59–60
revivals: Baltimore, 30, 41; Boston, 51;
   Buffalo, 41; Charlotte, 30; Chicago, 19,
   51, 60, 72; Elgin (IL), 45; Erie, 45;
   Garner (IA), 25–26; Knoxville (IA), 41;
   Memphis, 69; Mishawaka (IN), 104;
   New York City, 51–60; organization of,
   44–46; Perry (IA), 45; Philadelphia, 41,
   43, 46, 48–49; Pittsburgh, 41;
   Richmond (IN), 30, 41; Salida (CO), 46;
   Scranton (PA), 44; service format,
   36–39; Sterling (IL), 44; Steubenville
   (OH), 41, 48; Winston-Salem, 30. *See
   also* appendix A
Reynolds Presbyterian Orphanage, 6
Richmond, Indiana, 30, 41
Ritchart, Abraham, 133
Ritchart, Anna, 133
Rockefeller, John D., Jr., 33, 60
Rockefeller, John D., Sr., 43

Rodeheaver, Homer, 126; crowd control, 30, 36, 51, 53–54, 61; death of, 54; gifts from, 17, 49; reasons for leaving, 53–54; storytelling, 53, 68
Rodeheaver, Ruth, 126
Roper, Alvin W., 126
Roosevelt, Franklin Delano, 56–57
Roosevelt, Theodore, 56
Ruskin, John, 82

St. Louis Browns, 18
Salida, Colorado, 46
Sand, Robert Morrill, 126
Sandburg, Carl, 105
Sanders, Everett, 59
Sanders, Mae. See Mae Sanders Sunday
sawdust trail, 36–37
Saxe, Grace, 126
Scott, John, 12
Scranton, Pennsylvania revival, 44
Seibert, Fred, 126
Simmons, Amos, 131
Simmons, Mary Ann. See Mary Ann Sunday
Simmons, Rachel. See Rachel Simmons Hall
Sinatra, Frank, 72, 106
Snyder, Mary, 133
Social Gospel, 29, 65
Spiece, Joseph, 126
Spoor, George, 135
Spring Fountain Park, 78–79
Spurgeon, C. H., 65
Stephenson, Catherine, 131
Sterling, Illinois, 44
Steubenville, Ohio, 41, 48
Stickley, Gustav, 85, 89–90
Story County, Iowa, 1, 11
Stover, Dena P., 126
Stowell, infant, 130
Stowell, George, 130, 132
Strong, Vivian Bernice. See Vivian Bernice Strong Haines
Sundag, Heinrich. See Henry Sunday
Sunday, Albert Monroe, 2, 21, 130

Sunday, Alma Baine, 127, 128, 137
Sunday, Barnett, 131
Sunday, Catherine Stephenson. See Catherine Stephenson
Sunday, Christana, 132
Sunday, Cynthia, 128, 137
Sunday, Elisabeth, 132
Sunday, Ellen McDonald. See Ellen McDonald
Sunday, George Marquis, 17, 22, 100–103, 126, 128, 136
Sunday, George Marquis, Jr. "Marq," 127, 128, 137
Sunday, Harriet A., 131
Sunday, Harriet Corinne Mason, 127, 128, 136
Sunday, Helen Amelia Thompson ("Nell" or "Ma"), 126, 128, 134, 135; arts and crafts of, 8, 83, 89–90; birth of, 7; childhood of, 7–9; death of, 103, 127; designing of home, 86, 89, 96–100; education of, 7, 44–45; longevity of, 103; marriage to William A. Sunday, 7, 10, 15–16; role as Sunday organization business manager, 7–8, 44–54
Sunday, Helen Edith (Haines), 87, 90, 97, 100–101, 103, 129, 136
Sunday, Henry, 61, 128, 131, 132
Sunday, Henry, Jr., 132
Sunday, Howard Edward "Ed," 2, 6, 130
Sunday, Jacob, 132
Sunday, Jane, 128, 130, 131, 132
Sunday, Jane Geller. See Jane Geller
Sunday, Jeremiah, 131
Sunday, John, 128, 130, 131, 132
Sunday, John M., 103, 127, 128, 137
Sunday, Lillian, 128, 137
Sunday, Lurlyne P., 129, 136
Sunday, Mae Sanders, 128, 136
Sunday, Magdelena, 132
Sunday, Margaret Pratt. See Margaret Pratt
Sunday, Marquis Ashley, 128, 136, 137
Sunday, Mary Ann, 131
Sunday, Mary Jane "Jennie" Cory Heizer Stowell, 2, 3, 6, 130, 131, 132, 134

Sunday, Maryan, 127, 131, 132
Sunday, Mauryne Renee Reichard, 128, 136
Sunday, Millicent, 128, 136
Sunday, Nina, 128, 136
Sunday, Paul Thompson, 45, 87, 90, 98, 102–103, 129, 136
Sunday, Sarah Conner. *See* Sarah Conner
Sunday, Toni, 129, 136
Sunday, William A. (father of evangelist), 1–2, 6, 128, 130, 131, 132, 134
Sunday, William Ashley "Billy," 128, 134; apprenticeship under Chapman, 24–26; as a popular culture icon, 39–40, 106; birth of, 1; baseball career, 4, 12–17, 100; childhood of, 1–6; connections to business leaders, 33, 43; connections to Civil War veterans, 2, 4–5, 12; connections to political leaders, 56–60, 62, 72; conversion to Christianity, 9–10, 17–20; criticisms of, 30–32, 51, 74–75, 105–106; death of, 104; education of, 12, 14–16; emphasis on physical fitness and health, 26–28, 38–39, 74, 92; income, 20–22, 49–51, 60; involvement in First World War, 60–63; involvement in Prohibition/temperance, 24, 32, 36, 64, 68–75; marriage to Helen A. Thompson, 7, 10, 15–16; on amusements and dance, 56, 64–66, 70; on communist and socialist movements, 33, 56–59; on concept of sin, 59, 64–65, 68–70; on foreign immigration, 29, 32–33; on German heritage during war, 60–63; on labor reform, 33–34, 105–106; on rural/urban demographic changes, 32–33; on sex education, 56, 66–68; on women's suffrage, 56, 66–68; preaching style, 25–29, 36–44; relationships with family, 1–6, 96–103; research methods, 29–31, 57–58, 65–66, 69, 72, 74; statistical impact, 26, 40, 51; theological approach, 24–29, 32–36, 63–66; time in orphanage, 2–4, 6
Sunday, William Ashley, Jr. (son of evangelist), 45, 87, 98, 102–103, 126, 128, 136

tabernacle design, 36, 45–49, 60, 96
Taft, William H., 56
Thompson, Ada, 135
Thompson Dairy, 134
Thompson, Ellen Binnie, 7, 134, 135
Thompson, Flora Christine, 135
Thompson, Helen Amelia. *See* Helen Amelia Thompson Sunday
Thompson, James, 134
Thompson, Jennie, 135
Thompson, Louise, 134
Thompson, William F., Jr., 135
Thompson, William J., 5, 7, 134
Torrey, R. A., 65
Trotter, Melvin, 126
Truman, Harry S., 56

Van Winkle, J. R., 126

Walker, James E., 126
Walker, Sarah. *See* Sarah Walker Cory
Wanamaker, John, 33, 43
Ward, Isaac, 126
wars: Civil War, 2, 4–5, 12; First World War, 60–63; Second World War, 63, 103
Washington, George, 59
Welsh, John Wallace, 126
Whitbeck, Florence K., 126
Willard, Frances Elizabeth Caroline, 72
Williams, M. B., 46
Wilson, Woodrow, 56, 62
Winona Lake Christian Assembly and Bible Conference, 25, 77–80, 92
Winona Lake, Indiana, 78–80, 96
Winston-Salem, North Carolina revival, 30
Women's Christian Temperance Union, 43, 64, 72
Woods, Andrew, 133
Woods, Benjamin Ritchart, 133
Woods, Elizabeth Hall, 129, 131, 132, 133, 134
Woods, James Alexander, 133

Woods, John, 133
Woods, Joseph Hall, 133
Woods, Martha, 133
Woods, Mary Ann. *See* Mary Ann Woods Cory
Woods, Mary Ann (wife of Joseph Hall Woods), 133
Woods, Miranda, 133

Woods, Rachel, 133
Woods, Samuel, 129, 131, 132
Woods, Samuel, Jr., 133
Woods, Sarah S., 133
Woods, William, 132
Wright, Frank Lloyd, 87, 91

Y.M.C.A., 17, 19–25, 60, 63, 101, 105